Lecture Notes in Bioinformatics 10649

Subseries of Lecture Notes in Computer Science

More information about this series at http://www.springer.com/series/5381

Marcos Da Silveira · Cédric Pruski
Reinhard Schneider (Eds.)

Data Integration in the Life Sciences

12th International Conference, DILS 2017
Luxembourg, Luxembourg, November 14–15, 2017
Proceedings

 Springer

Editors
Marcos Da Silveira
Luxembourg Institute of Science
   and Technology
Esch-sur-Alzette
Luxembourg

Reinhard Schneider
Université du Luxembourg
Esch-sur-Alzette
Luxembourg

Cédric Pruski 🄸
Luxembourg Institute of Science
   and Technology
Esch-sur-Alzette
Luxembourg

ISSN 0302-9743   ISSN 1611-3349   (electronic)
Lecture Notes in Bioinformatics
ISBN 978-3-319-69750-5   ISBN 978-3-319-69751-2   (eBook)
https://doi.org/10.1007/978-3-319-69751-2

Library of Congress Control Number: 2017956781

LNCS Sublibrary: SL8 – Bioinformatics

Printed on acid-free paper

This Springer imprint is published by Springer Nature
The registered company is Springer International Publishing AG
The registered company address is: Gewerbestrasse 11, 6330 Cham, Switzerland

Preface

The 12th edition of the international conference on Data Integration in the Life Sciences (DILS), organized by the Luxembourg Institute of Science and Technology, was held in Hotel Parc-Bellevue during November 14–15, 2017, in Luxembourg. This year again, DILS 2017 brought together researchers (including students), developers, users, and practitioners involved in the integration, management, and analysis of heterogeneous data in the life sciences. DILS 2017 was a forum for computer scientists and members of different life science communities including bioinformatics, biodiversity, medicine, clinical health management, and pharmacy. This year, topics focused on life science data modeling and the management of life science datasets and models.

The call for papers attracted excellent contributions and a rigorous reviewing process was conducted to select the 10 best research and demo papers. Moreover, we had the pleasure to welcome two renowned speakers: Prof. Robert Stevens from the University of Manchester and Dr. Alex Bateman, Head of Protein Sequence Resources cluster of the European Bioinformatics Institute (EMBL-EBI). In his presentation, Prof. Stevens discussed the advances in the use of ontologies in the biomedical domain while Dr. Bateman discussed the UniProt Knowledge-Base, which has been providing data for protein sequence and function for over 30 years.

As the event co-chairs and editors of this volume, we would like to thank all authors who submitted papers, as well as the Program Committee members and additional reviewers for their excellent contribution in evaluating the submissions. Special thanks to Marylène Martin and the Luxembourg Institute of Science and Technology for their precious support in the organization of this event. Finally, we would like to thank Alfred Hofmann and his team at Springer for their cooperation and help in putting this volume together.

September 2017

Marcos Da Silveira
Cédric Pruski
Reinhard Schneider

Organization

Conference Chairs

Marcos Da Silveira   Luxembourg Institute of Science and Technology, Luxembourg

Cédric Pruski   Luxembourg Institute of Science and Technology, Luxembourg

Reinhard Schneider   University of Luxembourg, Luxembourg

Program Committee

Jose-Luis Ambite	University of Southern California, USA
Sarah Cohen-Boulakia	University of Paris-Sud, France
Stefan Darmoni	Rouen University Hospital, France
Juliette Dibie	AgroParisTech, France
Julio Cesar Dos Reis	University of Campinas, Brazil
Helena Galhardas	University of Lisbon, Portugal
Anika Gross	University of Leipzig, Germany
Wei Gu	University of Luxembourg, Luxembourg
Zhisheng Huang	Vrije Universiteit Amsterdam, The Netherlands
Graham Kemp	Chalmers University of Technology, Sweden
Andreas Kremer	ITTM, Luxembourg
Patrick Lambrix	Linköping University, Sweden
Ulf Leser	Humboldt-Universität zu Berlin, Germany
Dilvan Moreira	University of São Paulo, Brazil
Patrick Pirrotte	TGen, USA
Louiqa Raschid	University of Maryland, USA
Erhard Rahm	University of Leipzig, Germany
Patrick Ruch	University of Applied Sciences Western Switzerland, Switzerland
Venkata Satagopam	University of Luxembourg, Luxembourg
Annette ten Teije	Vrije Universiteit Amsterdam, The Netherlands
Christophe Trefois	University of Luxembourg, Luxembourg

Additional Reviewer

Ying-Chi Lin   University of Leipzig, Germany

Contents

Evaluating and Improving Annotation Tools
for Medical Forms

Ying-Chi Lin[1]([✉]), Victor Christen[1], Anika Groß[1], Silvio Domingos Cardoso[2,3],
Cédric Pruski[2], Marcos Da Silveira[2], and Erhard Rahm[1]

[1] Department of Computer Science, Universität Leipzig, Leipzig, Germany
{lin,christen,gross,rahm}@informatik.uni-leipzig.de
[2] LIST, Luxembourg Institute of Science and Technology,
Esch-sur-Alzette, Luxembourg
{silvio.cardoso,cedric.pruski,marcos.dasilveira}@list.lu
[3] LRI, University of Paris-Sud XI, Orsay, France

Abstract. The annotation of entities with concepts from standardized
terminologies and ontologies is of high importance in the life sciences
to enhance semantic interoperability, information retrieval and meta-
analysis. Unfortunately, medical documents such as clinical forms or
electronic health records are still rarely annotated despite the availability of some tools to automatically determine possible annotations. In this
study, we comparatively evaluate the quality of two such tools, cTAKES
and MetaMap, as well as of a recently proposed annotation approach
from our group for annotating medical forms. We also investigate how
to improve the match quality of the tools by post-filtering computed
annotations as well as by combining several annotation approaches.

Keywords: Annotation · Medical documents · Ontology · UMLS

1 Introduction

The interest for annotating datasets with concepts of controlled vocabularies,
terminologies or ontologies is increasing, especially in the biomedical domain.
Semantic annotations help to overcome typical data heterogeneity issues and
thus improve interoperability for different data providers and applications. For
instance, exchanging and analyzing the results from different clinical trials can
lead to new insights for diagnosis or treatment of diseases. Semantic annotations
of electronic health records (EHRs) showed to be valuable to identify adverse
effects of drugs and thus for developing better drugs [11,13]. NCI Metathesaurus
has been used to annotate semantically related entities in clinical documents to
achieve enhanced document retrieval [22]. Furthermore, annotations of publications help to better deal with the huge volume of research literature by enhancing
systems for automatically generating hypotheses from documents about relevant
factors, phenotypes, or biological processes [1].

In the healthcare sector there is a high and increasing number of documents
such as research publications, EHRs or case report forms (CRFs). For instance,

© Springer International Publishing AG 2017
M. Da Silveira et al. (Eds.): DILS 2017, LNBI 10649, pp. 1–16, 2017.
https://doi.org/10.1007/978-3-319-69751-2_1

there are almost 250,000 clinical studies registered on `ClinicalTrials.gov`. Dugas et al. estimate that more than 10 million different CRFs have been used so far [8], e.g., to document the medical history of patients or to evaluate eligibility criteria of probands of a study. Unfortunately, the vast majority of medical documents is still not annotated at all. For example, from the 11,000 forms and their 700,000 questions in the MDM portal[1], only about 1/7 have currently been annotated with concepts of the Unified Medical Language System (UMLS) Metathesaurus [14], the most widely used integrated vocabulary for clinical annotations [7]. The Metathesaurus currently contains more than 3.4 million concepts from over 200 controlled vocabularies and ontologies, such as ICD-10, SNOMED CT and MeSH. The huge number of documents, the use of natural language within the documents as well as the large complexity of biomedical ontologies such as UMLS make it challenging to find correct annotations for both automatic approaches as well as human experts. The most promising approach is thus to first apply a tool to automatically determine annotation candidates. A human expert can then select the final annotations from these candidates.

There exist several tools and approaches for such a semi-automatic annotation as well as a few initial evaluations of them [10,15,17,21]. In [21], the tools MetaMap, MGrep, ConceptMapper, cTAKES Dictionary Lookup Annotator and NOBLE Coder have been evaluated for annotating medical documents from the ShARe corpus[2] (containing clinical free-text notes from electrocardiogram and radiology reports) with concepts from the UMLS SNOMED-CT ontology. While the reported findings seem to indicate the usability of the tools the results cannot be generalized to different kinds of medical documents, such as other EHRs or CRFs.

In this study, we focus on the comparative evaluation of three tools/approaches for annotating CRFs and whether we can improve annotation quality by post-processing the tool results or by combining different approaches. We selected the tools *MetaMap* [2] and *cTAKES* [16] as well as our previous research approach [5] to which we refer here as *AnnoMap*. MetaMap is a well established tool and has been applied in many different types of tasks such as text mining, classification and question answering [2]. We chose cTAKES as it performed best in the mentioned evaluation study [21]. Specifically, we make the following contributions:

- We comparatively evaluate the three annotation tools based on the annotation of two kinds of English medical forms with the UMLS.
- We investigate to which degree the annotation results of cTAKES and MetaMap can be improved by additionally applying the group-based selection of annotation candidates from AnnoMap [5].
- We propose and evaluate annotation approaches combining the results generated by different tools in order to improve overall annotation quality.

---

[1] https://medical-data-models.org.
[2] https://sites.google.com/site/shareclefehealth/.

We first introduce the considered annotation tools and their combination in Sect. 2. We then describe the evaluation methodologies and analyze the results in Sect. 3. Finally, we summarize the findings and conclude.

2   Annotation Tools

The task of *annotation* or *concept recognition* has as input a set of documents $D = \{d_1, d_2, ..., d_n\}$, e.g., publications, EHRs, or CRFs, to annotate as well as the ontology ON from which the concepts for annotation are to be found. The goal is to determine for each relevant document fragment *df* such as sentences or questions in medical forms the set of its most precisely describing ontology concepts. The annotation result is a set of so-called *annotation mappings* $\mathcal{AM}_{d_i, ON} = \{(df_j, \{c_1, ..., c_m\}) | df_j \in d_i, c_k \in ON\}$ where each mapping refers to one document d_i and consists of the associations between the document fragments and its set of annotating concepts.

Several tools for the automatic annotation of documents in the life sciences have been developed in the last years. Such *annotators* can be generally categorized into dictionary-based and machine learning-based approaches [3]. The learning-based approaches typically require a training corpus which is rarely available for a new set of documents to annotate. As a result, the more general-purpose dictionary-based approaches are mostly favored. To speedup the annotation process, they typically create a dictionary for the ontology (e.g., UMLS) to be used for finding annotating concepts. Examples of such tools include MetaMap [2], NCBO Annotator [6], IndexFinder [24], MedLEE [9], ConceptMapper [20], NOBLE Coder [21], cTAKES [16] as well as our own AnnoMap approach [5]. We further developed an extension of AnnoMap utilizing previous annotations which can be seen as a special kind of training data [4].

In this study, we evaluate three annotation tools and their combination: MetaMap, cTAKES and AnnoMap. Table 1 summarizes the main features of these annotators w.r.t. three phases: preprocessing, candidate generation and postprocessing. The preprocessing phase is divided into an offline and an online step. The offline step is devoted to generating the dictionary for the ontology with indexed entries for the concepts to support fast lookup. The online step is used to preprocess the input documents by using NLP approaches. In the candidate generation phase, the annotation candidates for each text fragment are identified by using a dictionary lookup strategy or a fuzzy matching based on similarity functions. Finally, the postprocessing phase selects the annotations from the annotation candidates.

In the following, we discuss the three tools in more detail. At the end, we discuss possible combinations of the individual tools aiming at improving the annotation quality compared to the use of only one approach.

Table 1. Components and functions of MetaMap, cTAKES and AnnoMap. POS: Part of Speech, LCS: Longest Common Substring

Tool	Ontology prepocessing	Form preprocessing	Candidate generation	Post-processing
MetaMap	dictionary construction (UMLS, SPECIALIST lexicon)	sentence detector, tokenizer, POS tagger/filter, shallow parser, variant generation (static/dynamic), abbreviation identifier	dictionary lookup (first word)	word sense disambiguation, score-based filtering
cTAKES	dictionary construction (UMLS)	sentence detector, tokenizer, POS tagger/filter, shallow parser, variantgeneration (dynamic)	dictionary lookup (rare word)	-
AnnoMap	-	tokenizer, POS tagger/filter, TF/IDF computation	fuzzy match (TF/IDF, Trigram, LCS)	threshold-based, group-based

2.1 MetaMap

MetaMap was originally developed to improve the retrieval of bibliographic documents such as MEDLINE citations [2]. It is designed to map biomedical mentions to concepts in UMLS Metathesaurus. MetaMap is based on a dictionary-lookup by using several sources such as UMLS itself as well as SPECIALIST lexicon. The SPECIALIST lexicon contains syntactic, morphological, and spelling variations of commonly occurring English words and biomedical terms of UMLS [14]. The input text is first split into sentences and further parsed into phrases. These phrases are the basic units for the variant generation and candidate retrieval. MetaMap provides several configurations for the lookup of annotation candidates per phrase such as *gap* allowance, *ignore* word order, and *dynamic* as well as *static* variant generation. For each annotation candidate MetaMap computes a complex score function considering linguistic metrics [2] for each phrase of a sentence. The final result is determined by the combination of candidates maximizing the aggregated score. MetaMap also provides an optional postprocessing step, word sense disambiguation (WSD), for cases when the final result has several Metathesaurus concepts with similar scores. WSD selects the concept that is semantically most consistent with the surrounding text [12].

2.2 cTAKES

cTAKES[3] is built on the Apache UIMA framework[4] providing a standardized architecture for processing unstructured data. To annotate medical documents, cTAKES provides several components for specifying preprocessing and lookup

---

[3] Clinical Text Analysis and Knowledge Extraction System http://ctakes.apache.org.
[4] Unstructured Information Management Architecture [16] https://uima.apache.org.

strategies. The components are used to define customized annotation pipelines where each component uses the intermediate output of the previous component as input. In addition to general components used in a default pipeline, cTAKES offers domain-specific components such as for the classification of smoking status [19], the extraction of drug side effects [18], and coreference resolution [23].

In the following, we describe the default pipeline with its components. During (offline) preprocessing, an ontology dictionary is built where each property of a concept becomes an entry in the dictionary. The rarest word of an entry is used to index it for fast lookup. The rareness of a word is based on the global occurrence frequency in the ontology. For the (online) preprocessing of the input documents, cTAKES uses the following components: sentence boundary detector, customized part of speech (POS) tagger and a lexical variant generator. The model of the POS tagger is trained for medical entities based on clinical data since general POS taggers do not cover domain-specific characteristics such as abbreviations. In general, medical entity mentions within documents can be different according to the name and synonyms of concepts. Therefore, cTAKES applies a lexical variant generator (LVG) to transform differently inflected forms, conjugations or alphabetic cases to a canonical form for improved comparability. While cTAKES permits the addition of customized postprocessing steps to the pipeline such strategies are not part of the cTAKES core project.

2.3 AnnoMap

AnnoMap implements a general approach for annotating documents with concepts of arbitrary ontologies. In the current version, it does not create a dictionary of the ontology during preprocessing for fast lookup but directly searches in the ontology for finding suitable annotations. In the preprocessing step, the concept entries and the documents are normalized by applying several text transformation functions such as lower case, stop word elimination, POS filtering or removing characters that are not alpha-numeric. For candidate generation, AnnoMap loads the ontology into main memory and applies a general match approach by comparing each document fragment with each ontology concept. Matching is based on the combined similarity score from different string similarity functions, in particular TF/IDF, Trigram and LCS (longest common substring) similarity. AnnoMap retains all annotation candidates with a score above a given threshold δ. This corresponds to a fuzzy matching that tolerates name variations and typos which might not be the case for the lookup techniques of MetaMap and cTAKES.

During postprocessing, AnnoMap filters the candidates of a document fragment with a *group-based selection strategy* that aims at keeping only the best annotations for groups of similar annotation candidates. Figure 1 illustrates this selection approach for the candidates of two document fragments (e.g. CRF questions) df_1 and df_2. The candidates of a document fragment are first grouped or clustered based on the mutual (string) similarity of the annotating concepts. For groups of highly similar candidates, the approach then only retains the one with the highest annotation score. In the example, concepts c_1 and c_2 represent a group for df_1 and c_3 and c_4 form a group for df_2. From these groups, c_1 and c_4 have the highest score and are retained while candidates c_2 and c_3 are removed from the result.

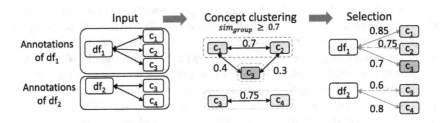

Fig. 1. Example for the group-based selection strategy

The described group-based selection can also be applied to postprocess the results of the tools MetaMap and cTAKES and we will evaluate the effectiveness of such a combined strategy. Furthermore, we can combine the three tools as described in the next subsection.

2.4 Combining Different Tools

The considered tools follow different approaches for finding annotations that may complement each other. Hence, it is promising to combine the results of the individual approaches to hopefully improve overall annotation quality, e.g., to improve recall (find more correct annotations) or/and precision (eliminate less likely annotations that are not confirmed by two or more tools). For combining the annotation results of two or more tools we follow three simple approaches: *union*, *intersection* and *majority*. The *union* approach includes the annotations from any tool to improve recall while *intersection* only preserves annotations found by all tools for improved precision. The *majority* approach includes the annotations found by a majority of tools, e.g., by at least two of three tools. There are further variations for combining the approaches by differentiating whether the proposed group-based selection is applied before or after the combination (aggregation) of the individual tool results. The two resulting workflows, wf_1 and wf_2, are illustrated in Fig. 2. In the first case (wf_1) we combine postprocessed annotation results after we have applied group-based selection to the results of the respective tools. For wf_2, we aggregate the results without individual postprocessing but apply group-based selection only on the combined annotation result.

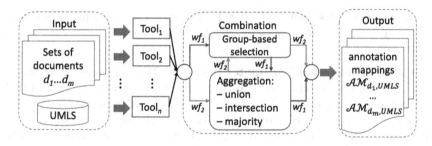

Fig. 2. Workflows for combining the annotation results of different tools. Workflow wf_1 first applies group-based selection for each tool and then combines the selection results. Workflow wf_2 first combines the annotation results of each tool and then selects the final annotations on the combined result.

3   Evaluation and Results

We now comparatively evaluate the three annotation tools MetaMap, cTAKES and AnnoMap and their combinations using two sets of medical forms and the UMLS Metathesaurus. We first describe our experimental setup including the datasets and tool configurations. We then evaluate the annotation results for single tools and the additional use of group-based selection (Sect. 3.2) as well as for the combination of two or three tools (Sect. 3.3). Sect. 3.4 summarizes the results. The evaluation focuses on the standard metrics *recall, precision* and their harmonic mean *F-measure* as the main indicator for annotation quality.

3.1   Experimental Setup

Document Sets and Ontologies: We use two datasets with medical forms (CRFs) from the MDM portal that have also been used in previous annotation evaluations [4,5] and for which a reference mapping exists: a dataset with forms on *eligibility criteria* (EC) and a dataset with *quality assurance* (QA) forms.

The EC dataset contains 25 forms with 310 manually annotated questions. These forms are used to recruit patients in clinical trials for diseases such as epilepsy or hemophilia. The QA dataset has 24 standardized forms with 543 annotated questions used in cardio-vascular procedures. The number of annotations in the reference mappings is 541 for EC and 589 for QA. The previous evaluations [4,5] showed that it is very challenging to correctly identify all annotations for these datasets.

To annotate we use UMLS version 2014AB that was used for the manual annotation. We include five vocabularies: UMLS Metathesaurus, NCI (National Cancer Institute) Thesaurus, MedDRA[5], OAC-CHV[6], and SNOMED-CT_US[7], covering most annotations in the manually determined reference mappings.

---

[5] Medical Dictionary for Regulatory Activities.

[6] Open-access and Collaborative (OAC) Consumer Health Vocabulary (CHV).

[7] US Extension to Systematized Nomenclature of Medicine-Clinical Terms.

Since we use different subsets of UMLS in this paper and in the previous studies [5], the results are not directly comparable.

Tool Configuration and Parameter Settings: The considered tools provide a large spectrum of possible configurations making it difficult to find suitable parameter settings. To limit the scope of the comparative evaluation and still allow a fair comparison we analyzed the influence of different parameters in a preparatory evaluation to arrive at default configurations achieving reasonable annotation quality per tool.

Table 2 lists the considered parameters for cTAKES, MetaMap and AnnoMap. For MetaMap, we found that the best *scoreFilter* values are (700/800/900) for EC and also 1000 for QA. *WSD* delivered significant better F-measures than *default* only for the EC dataset, for which *dynVar* does not provide noticeable improvements. For QA, *dynVar* as well as *gaps* could produce better results than *default* but the results were inferior to the use of *WSD* when we combine several tools. Hence, we omit the results of *gaps* and *dynVar* and focus on MetaMap results for *default* and *WSD* with different *scoreFilter* values.

For cTAKES, using *longestMatch* results in improved precision and F-measure. While *overlap* is supposed to increase recall, this is not the case for our datasets so that we exclude experiments using this parameter. For AnnoMap,

Table 2. Tested parameters in MetaMap, cTAKES and AnnoMap

Parameter	Description
MetaMap	
gaps	allows gaps between tokens
dynVar	generates variants dynamically rather than only lookup table
WSD	enables word sense disambiguation
scoreFilter	sets the threshold to filter out mapping candidates. MetaMap score values range between 0–1000 (tested values: 700/800/900 for EC and 700/800/900/1000 for QA)
wordOrder	matches also terms in different orders
derivVar	specifies which type of derivational variations to be used (tested settings: default/none/all). Default uses only derivational variations between adjectives and nouns
cTAKES	
overlap	allows matches on discontiguous spans
longestMatch	returns only the concept with the longest matched span
AnnoMap	
threshold δ	sets the minimum similarity for filtering annotation candidates (tested values: 0.6–0.8 with 0.5 interval)

we tested the thresholds δ ranging from 0.6 and 0.8 based on our previous investigation in [5]. We apply the best-performing results in the experiments, i.e., $\delta = 0.7$ for EC and $\delta = 0.75$ for QA.

To use the group-based selection strategy (Sect. 2.3) for the tools cTAKES and MetaMap, we need a score per annotation candidate to select the one with the highest score from a group of similar candidates. For MetaMap, we use the generated scores divided by 1000 (to obtain a value between 0 to 1) for this purpose. Since cTAKES does not determine any score, we calculate a linguistic similarity between each question and its matched concept using Soft TF/IDF as the annotation score.

3.2 Evaluation of Single Tools and Use of Group-Based Selection

We first assess the annotation quality for the single approaches cTAKES, Meta-Map and AnnoMap without and with the additional use of group-based selection. Figure 3 presents the results for the datasets (a) EC and (b) QA with different parameter settings. AnnoMap with group-based selection achieves the highest F-measure among all tools/parameter settings for both EC (39.5%) and QA (56.1%). Group-based selection is an integral part of AnnoMap but for comparison we also show AnnoMap results without this selection method. We observe

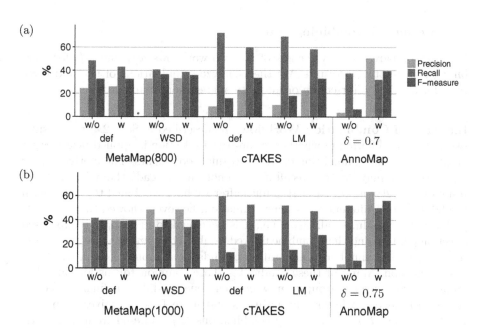

Fig. 3. Annotation quality of MetaMap, cTAKES and AnnoMap without (w/o) and with (w) group-based selection in datasets (a) EC and (b) QA. The MetaMap results refer to the best-performing *scoreFilter* setting.
def: *default* setting, WSD: Word Sense Disambiguation, LM: *longestMatch*

that group-based selection dramatically increases precision by filtering out a large amount of false positives after initial candidate generation in AnnoMap (e.g., from 8,573 to only 170 for QA). Overall, AnnoMap achieves the best precision among all tools in both datasets (50.6% for EC and 63.5% for QA).

The highest recall values are obtained by cTAKES default (def) without group-based selection (72.5% for EC and 60.1% for QA), at the expense of very low precision values (less than 9%) and thus poor F-measure. Applying the *longestMatch* (LM) function decreases the number of false positives by about 1/4 (e.g., from 4,407 to 3,164 for QA) and slightly improves precision to about 10%. Significantly more effective is the proposed extension of cTAKES with group-based selection which improves precision as well as F-measure by about a factor of two for both datasets. As a result, the best cTAKES F-measure results, 33.4% for EC and 28.8% for QA, are achieved with cTAKES(def) with group-based selection.

MetaMap achieves better F-measure results than cTAKES especially when applying WSD with a maximum of 36.4% for EC (with *scoreFilter* = 800) and 40.2% for QA (*scoreFilter* = 1000). In contrast to cTAKES, the use of group-based selection did not improve annotation quality since MetaMap itself already filters similar annotation candidates based on their scores within phrases (Sect. 2.1). Applying WSD improved F-measure over the default strategy of MetaMap by up to 4% by further filtering the annotation candidates.

3.3   Results of Combining Tools

We first compare the effectiveness of the two workflows wf_1 and wf_2 for combining the annotation results. We then analyze combinations of two and three tools for a union, intersection or majority aggregation of annotations.

Influence of Combination Workflow: As described in Sect. 2.4, we consider two workflows differing in whether group-based selection is applied before (wf_1) or after (wf_2) the combination of the individual tool results. The motivation for wf_2 is that we may improve recall if we do not filter already the individual tool results but postpone the filter step until after we have combined the annotation candidates from different tools. Our evaluation, however, showed that wf_1 outperforms wf_2 in almost all cases, i.e., it is beneficial to first apply group-based selection per tool and then combine filtered results. For a *union* aggregation, wf_2 results in a large number of annotation candidates as input to the final group-based selection. Many of these candidates share common tokens and are thus grouped into the same group from which only one candidate is finally selected. Hence, wf_2 leads to fewer true positives and more false negatives than wf_1. For the *intersection* or *majority* combinations, wf_2 suffered from more false positives and such a reduced precision compared to wf_1 which can not be outweighed by a slightly higher recall. Given the superiority of wf_1 we will only present results for this approach in the following.

Combining Two Tools: For two tools, we support a union or intersection of the individual results (the majority approach corresponds to intersection here). We have three possible tool combinations for which the average results on annotation quality are shown in Fig. 4. The averages are taken over all configurations of a tool while the vertical bars (*variance bars*) denote the spectrum between the minimal and maximal result per combination. As expected, we see that the *union* combinations achieve high recall values while *intersection* leads to increased precision over the single tools. More importantly, we note that *intersection* consistently leads to improved F-measure compared to the *union* combination indicating that the improvements on precision are more decisive than the recall increases. The large variance bars for some combinations reflect a substantial influence of some parameter settings such as the *scoreFilter* value of MetaMap.

For the EC dataset (Fig. 4a), the best F-measure of 42.1% is achieved for the (intersection) combination of MetaMap and cTAKES. This combination also outperforms all single tools including AnnoMap (39.5%). The combinations AM-CT and AM-MM cannot reach the F-measure of AnnoMap but outperform the single tools cTAKES and MetaMap, respectively, mainly due to an improved precision (ranging from 62.8% to 81.6%).

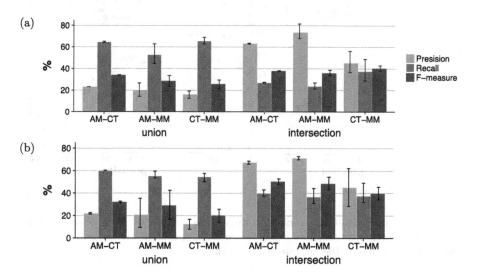

Fig. 4. Average annotation quality of combining two tools for different parameter settings with datasets (a) EC and (b) QA. Variance bars show the maximum and minimum quality values. The results are obtained using wf_1.

For the QA dataset (Fig. 4b), the highest F-measure (54.4%) for combining two tools is obtained by intersecting the results of AnnoMap and MetaMap (700/def). While this result is slightly lower than for AnnoMap alone (56.1%) it substantially outperforms the F-measure of MetaMap alone (40.2%). Similarly, the combination AM-CT leads to a strong F-measure improvement compared to cTAKES alone. By contrast, the combination CT-MM is less effective than for EC but still improves on the single tools.

Combining Three Tools: For three tools, we can apply three aggregation approaches (union, intersection, majority) and have many combinations depending on which configuration per tool we select. We therefore use now precision-recall plots in Fig. 5 to present the results for the (a) EC and (b) QA datasets. The curves inside these plots refer to different F-measure values (f). Both plots show that the results of different aggregation methods form three distinctive clusters. The combinations based on a *union* aggregation have the best recall but the lowest precision while the *intersection* combinations have opposite characteristics. The *majority* combinations are able to better balance recall and precision and lie therefore in-between the two other approaches and achieve mostly the best F-measure values.

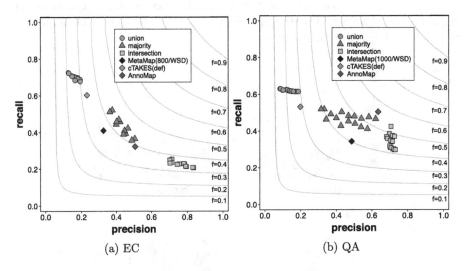

Fig. 5. Annotation quality of combining three tools using wf_1. Each point refers to a union, intersection or majority combination for a specific cTAKES and MetaMap configuration, as well as the best single tool results.

For EC, all *majority* combinations outperformed each single tool in terms of F-measure (Fig. 5a). This is because the combinations improved recall over MetaMap and AnnoMap and precision over cTAKES. The best F-measure (44.3%) is obtained by the *majority* of AnnoMap, cTAKES (def) and MetaMap (800/WSD), i.e., with the configurations for cTAKES and MetaMap that performed best when using these tools alone. As for two tool combinations, the *union* approach achieves always lower F-measure than with *intersection*.

For the QA dataset (Fig. 5b), the best F-measure (53.2%) is achieved by the *majority* aggregation of the combination AnnoMap, cTAKES (def) and

MetaMap (1000/WSD). Again, these are the best performing QA configurations of the single tools. The single tool results for both cTAKES and MetaMap are outperformed by all combinations of three tools using either *majority* or *intersection*. However, different from the EC dataset the F-measure of AnnoMap alone can not be topped by the combined schemes. This is because recall decreased compared to AnnoMap alone indicating that AnnoMap can determine many valid annotation candidates that are not found by another tool to build a majority. The precision for *majority* also differs over a large range (31.4%–62.1%) mainly due to a strong dependency on the *scoreFilter* of MetaMap.

3.4   Result Summary

The presented evaluation showed that the annotation quality of existing tools such as cTAKES and AnnoMap can be substantially improved by the proposed combinations such as adding a group-based selection of annotation candidates and aggregating the results of different tools. Most effective is the use of both optimizations, i.e., the use of group-based selection and the aggregation of results from two or more tools. In this case, it is better to first apply group-based selection per tool before aggregating the results (combination workflow wf_1). From the considered aggregation strategies, *intersection* performs best for two tools and *majority* for three tools. For the EC and QA datasets, the single tool performance of cTAKES is lower than for MetaMap and the research approach AnnoMap. However, by applying the combination strategies these differences can be reduced to a large degree.

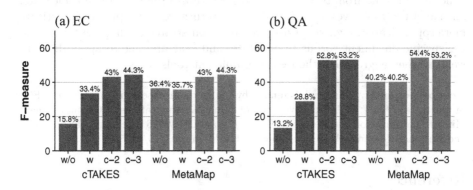

Fig. 6. Summarizing F-measure results for cTAKES and MetaMap and the proposed combinations for the (a) EC and (b) QA datasets. The combinations are w/o: without group-based selection, w: with group-based selection, c-2: best results from combining two tools, c-3: best results from combining three tools. For EC, the c-2 configuration is cTAKES (def) with MetaMap (700/def), and for c-3: AnnoMap with cTAKES (def) and MetaMap (800/WSD). For QA, the c-2 configurations are cTAKES (def) with AnnoMap and MetaMap (700/def) with AnnoMap. For c-3: AnnoMap with cTAKES (def) and MetaMap (1000/WSD).

Figure 6 summarizes the impact of the proposed combination strategies on F-measure for cTAKES and MetaMap. We observe that the F-measure of cTAKES can be dramatically improved (about a factor 3–4) for both datasets. Adding group-based selection alone already doubles F-measure. Combining cTAKES with MetaMap or AnnoMap further improves F-measure noticeably. For MetaMap with the WSD option, the additional use of group-based selection is not useful but the aggregation with other tools also improved F-measure substantially. Interestingly, most improvements can already be achieved by combining only two tools. AnnoMap is the best-performing single tool and its combination with other tools generally improves annotation quality for these tools. The quality for AnnoMap itself can be topped for the EC dataset by a majority combination of all three tools but not for the QA dataset. We therefore see a need to investigate strategies to further improve annotation quality for tools such as AnnoMap.

4   Conclusions

The large-scale annotation of documents in healthcare such as medical forms or EHRs is of high benefit but still in an early stage. In this paper, we comprehensively evaluated the quality of three existing annotation tools (MetaMap, cTAKES and AnnoMap) for real-world medical forms and proposed several combination approaches to improve their effectiveness and thus their practical applicability. We showed that post-processing the annotation results with group-based selection of annotation candidates as well as the aggregation of annotation results from two or more tools can substantially increase F-measure, for one of the tools even by a factor 3–4. In future work, we plan to investigate more sophisticated, e.g., supervised combination strategies that are tailored to the specific document corpus to annotate, and that are able to apply different weights when aggregating the results of different tools.

Acknowledgment. This work is funded by the German Research Foundation (DFG) (grant RA 497/22-1, "ELISA - Evolution of Semantic Annotations"), German Federal Ministry of Education and Research (BMBF) (grant 031L0026, "Leipzig Health Atlas") and National Research Fund Luxembourg (FNR) (grant C13/IS/5809134).

References

1. Abedi, V., Zand, R., Yeasin, M., Faisal, F.E.: An automated framework for hypotheses generation using literature. BioData Min. **5**(1), 13 (2012)
2. Aronson, A.R., Lang, F.M.: An overview of MetaMap: historical perspective and recent advances. J. Am. Med. Inform. Assoc. **17**(3), 229–236 (2010)
3. Campos, D., Matos, S., Oliveira, J.: Current methodologies for biomedical named entity recognition. In: Biological Knowledge Discovery Handbook: Preprocessing, Mining, and Postprocessing of Biological Data, pp. 839–868 (2013)

4. Christen, V., Groß, A., Rahm, E.: A reuse-based annotation approach for medical documents. In: Groth, P., Simperl, E., Gray, A., Sabou, M., Krötzsch, M., Lecue, F., Flöck, F., Gil, Y. (eds.) ISWC 2016. LNCS, vol. 9981, pp. 135–150. Springer, Cham (2016). doi:10.1007/978-3-319-46523-4_9

5. Christen, V., Groß, A., Varghese, J., Dugas, M., Rahm, E.: Annotating medical forms using UMLS. In: Ashish, N., Ambite, J.-L. (eds.) DILS 2015. LNCS, vol. 9162, pp. 55–69. Springer, Cham (2015). doi:10.1007/978-3-319-21843-4_5

6. Dai, M., Shah, N.H., Xuan, W., Musen, M.A., Watson, S.J., Athey, B.D., Meng, F., et al.: An efficient solution for mapping free text to ontology terms. In: AMIA Summit on Translational Bioinformatics 21 (2008)

7. Doan, S., Conway, M., Phuong, T.M., Ohno-Machado, L.: Natural language processing in biomedicine: a unified system architecture overview. In: Trent, R. (ed.) Clinical Bioinformatics. Methods in Molecular Biology (Methods and Protocols), vol 1168, pp. 275–294. Humana Press, New York (2014)

8. Dugas, M., Neuhaus, P., Meidt, A., Doods, J., Storck, M., Bruland, P., Varghese, J.: Portal of medical data models: information infrastructure for medical research and healthcare. Database: The Journal of Biological Databases and Curation p. bav121 (2016)

9. Friedman, C., Shagina, L., Lussier, Y., Hripcsak, G.: Automated encoding of clinical documents based on natural language processing. J. Am. Med. Inform. Assoc. **11**(5), 392–402 (2004)

10. Funk, C., Baumgartner, W., Garcia, B., Roeder, C., Bada, M., Cohen, K.B., Hunter, L.E., Verspoor, K.: Large-scale biomedical concept recognition: an evaluation of current automatic annotators and their parameters. BMC Bioinform. **15**(1), 1–29 (2014)

11. Heinemann, F., Huber, T., Meisel, C., Bundschus, M., Leser, U.: Reflection of successful anticancer drug development processes in the literature. Drug Discovery Today **21**(11), 1740–1744 (2016)

12. Humphrey, S.M., Rogers, W.J., Kilicoglu, H., Demner-Fushman, D., Rindflesch, T.C.: Word sense disambiguation by selecting the best semantic type based on Journal Descriptor Indexing: Preliminary experiment. J. Am. Soc. Inform. Sci. Technol. **57**(1), 96–113 (2006)

13. LePendu, P., Iyer, S., Fairon, C., Shah, N.H., et al.: Annotation analysis for testing drug safety signals using unstructured clinical notes. J. Biomed. Semant. **3**(S-1), S5 (2012)

14. McCray, A.T., Srinivasan, S., Browne, A.C.: Lexical methods for managing variation in biomedical terminologies. In: Proceedings of the Annual Symposium on Computer Application in Medical Care, pp. 235–239 (1994)

15. Oellrich, A., Collier, N., Smedley, D., Groza, T.: Generation of silver standard concept annotations from biomedical texts with special relevance to phenotypes. PLoS ONE **10**(1), e0116040 (2015)

16. Savova, G.K., Masanz, J.J., Ogren, P.V., Zheng, J., Sohn, S., Kipper-Schuler, K.C., Chute, C.G.: Mayo clinical Text Analysis and Knowledge Extraction System (cTAKES): architecture, component evaluation and applications. J. Am. Med. Inform. Assoc. **17**(5), 507–513 (2010)

17. Shah, N.H., Bhatia, N., Jonquet, C., Rubin, D., Chiang, A.P., Musen, M.A.: Comparison of concept recognizers for building the open biomedical annotator. BMC Bioinform. **10**(Suppl. 9), S14–S14 (2009)

18. Sohn, S., Kocher, J.P.A., Chute, C.G., Savova, G.K.: Drug side effect extraction from clinical narratives of psychiatry and psychology patients. J. Am. Med. Inform. Assoc. **18**(Suppl. 1), i144–i149 (2011)

19. Sohn, S., Savova, G.K.: Mayo clinic smoking status classification system: extensions and improvements. In: AMIA Annual Symposium Proceedings, pp. 619–623 (2009)
20. Tanenblatt, M.A., Coden, A., Sominsky, I.L.: The ConceptMapper approach to named entity recognition. In: Proceedings of 7th Language Resources and Evaluation Conference (LREC), pp. 546–551 (2010)
21. Tseytlin, E., Mitchell, K., Legowski, E., Corrigan, J., Chavan, G., Jacobson, R.S.: NOBLE-Flexible concept recognition for large-scale biomedical natural language processing. BMC Bioinform. **17**(1), 32 (2016)
22. University of Pittsburgh: TIES-Text Information Extraction System (2017). http://ties.dbmi.pitt.edu/
23. Zheng, J., Chapman, W.W., Miller, T.A., Lin, C., Crowley, R.S., Savova, G.K.: A system for coreference resolution for the clinical narrative. J. Am. Med. Inform. Assoc. **19**(4), 660 (2012)
24. Zou, Q., Chu, W.W., Morioka, C., Leazer, G.H., Kangarloo, H.: Indexfinder: a knowledge-based method for indexing clinical texts. In: AMIA Annual Symposium Proceedings, pp. 763–767 (2003)

A Simple Tool to Enrich Clinical Trial Data with Multiontology-Based Conceptual Tags

Holger Stenzhorn[1,2(✉)]

[1] Chair of Methods in Medical Informatics,
University of Tübingen, Tübingen, Germany
holger.stenzhorn@uni-tuebingen.de
[2] Faculty of Medicine, Saarland University, Homburg, Saar, Germany

1 Introduction

The use of ontologies to ease planning and execution of clinical trials and the handling of the resulting data has been proposed in various forms over the past years ranging from dedicated ontologies to ontology-driven software. ObTiMA [11] is of the latter type and provides a complete web-based clinical trial management system which allows to define all data collection forms and items visually and then automatically generates both user interface and the database to enter patient data. Using the system in several projects proofed its ontological base as useful and powerful but also revealed four major issues:

- The initial focus for using ontological concepts was on semantically defining forms for data collection and the contained questions. Only little attention was paid on enabling the automatic or manual enrichment of other trial items.
- Despite the visual design of those forms, its user interface to semantically define questions (based on an ontology tree) was judged as difficult to use by clinical experts without ontology experts (and thus time-consuming and error-prone).
- The concepts could only be selected from a single ontology which was hard-coded into the system (first the ACGT Master Ontology [2], later (after some re-coding) the Health Data Ontology Trunk [9]). Thus established ontologies, like NCI Thesaurus [8] or SNOMED CT [10] could not be employed.
- Albeit trial data could be exported in standard CDISC ODM [3] extended with ontological concepts, no standard tool was capable to interpret this additional information and an export in RDF format for further processing was missing.

To target those issues, an extensive reengineering took place and is described in detail below: Now, any external ontology can be imported and its concepts used to specify additional data for all logical parts of a trial. A simpler user interface hides the inherent complexity of the ontologies and finally, all trial data can now be exported via RDF.

2 Ontology Management

The restriction to a single, hard-coded ontology was lifted and the possibility to import and use ontologies dynamically at runtime was introduced. Figure 1

© Springer International Publishing AG 2017
M. Da Silveira et al. (Eds.): DILS 2017, LNBI 10649, pp. 17–21, 2017.
https://doi.org/10.1007/978-3-319-69751-2_2

| Acronym ^ | Name ◇ | Namespace | | Enabled ◇ |
		Prefix ◇	IRI ◇	
ChEBI	Chemical Entities of Biological Interest	obo	http://purl.obolibrary.org/obo/	✓
CTCAE	Common Terminology Criteria for Adverse Events	ctcae	http://ncicb.nci.nih.gov/xml/owl/EVS/ctcae.owl#	✓
DO	Disease Ontology	obo	http://purl.obolibrary.org/obo/	✓
FMA	Foundational Model of Anatomy	fma	http://purl.org/sig/ont/fma/	✓
GO	Gene Ontology	obo	http://purl.obolibrary.org/obo/	✓
LOINC	Logical Observation Identifiers Names and Codes	loinc	http://loinc.org/owl#	✓
MedDRA	Medical Dictionary for Regulatory Activities	meddra	http://purl.bioontology.org/ontology/MEDDRA/	✓
NCIt	NCI Thesaurus	ncit	http://ncicb.nci.nih.gov/xml/owl/EVS/Thesaurus.owl#	✓
OBI	Ontology for Biomedical Investigations	obo	http://purl.obolibrary.org/obo/	✓
SNOMED-CT	Systematized Nomenclature of Medicine Clinical Terms	snomed-ct	http://snomed.info/	✓

« ‹ 1 2 › » 10 ▾

Add   Reload All

Fig. 1. List of the ontologies currently loaded in the system.

presents an (example) excerpt of all currently loaded ontologies. To add an ontology, the user simply clicks on the respective button and provides in a pop-up dialog (optional) acronym, name, namespace, (optional) description and source location of the ontology where the latter can either be any remote Web location or a local file reference (e.g. if the ontology artifacts are too large or not openly available). During the loading process, the ontologies are scanned for concepts and their respective identifiers and (possibly multilingual) labels are stored in a Lucene-based index [1] for performant subsequent retrieval. The ontologies can be either in OWL format or a text file with each line containing the concept identifier and label. (To extract this data, a regular expression has to be provided).

After the import, the ontologies and their concepts are immediately available system-wide and can be added to existing trials or used when creating new ones. Within a trial it is then possible to select the relevant ontologies, as shown in Fig. 2, so that users in that trial are only presented with the concepts from those ontologies (and irrelevant concepts from others are hidden).

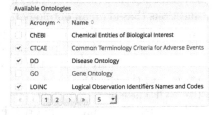

Fig. 2. Ontologies selected for being used within a trial.

3   Conceptual Tagging

The tagging of the different trial elements with concepts is realized as autocomplete field widgets with drop-down lists of all matching concepts. This means that in order to find a suitable concept, the user does not have to navigate through complex ontology trees but simply types one or more terms (or subterms) in the text field and all ontologies selected for the trial are searched for the fitting concepts where their labels contains all elements of the entered query. Note that the drop-down lists are updated dynamically when typing or erasing characters in the field. (To keep the user interface highly responsive even with long queries and several large ontologies at once, this is realized by employing the Lucene index – cf. above.) The concepts displayed are grouped according to their source ontology and for each concept its identifier and all attached (possibly multilingual) labels are shown too, cf. Figs. 3, 4 and 5.

Fig. 3. Concepts from multiple ontologies matching the terms in the query.

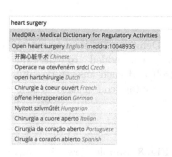

Fig. 4. Single matching concept with various labels in several languages.

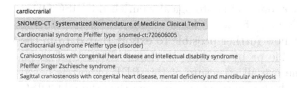

Fig. 5. Single concept with alternative labels.

Note again that this interface is uniform for all "taggable" trial elements. A concrete example is the creation of a question about a patient's gender with two answer possiblities. In here, concepts for *Gender* are chosen from both NCI Thesaurus and SNOMED CT to tag the question and its answer possibilities *Male* and *Female*, see Figs. 6 and 7. Note that this is part of the trial setup process where all necessary aspects, including the ontology-based tags are visible. But when patient data is entered during the trial execution, all tags are hidden from the users (e.g. trial nurses) as they are concerned with a quick and simple data entry but not with any ontological representations, see Fig. 8. (Yet in the background, all questions/answers are still linked to their defined tags.).

Fig. 6. Definition of a question with concepts/tags added to the question itself and each answer possibility (marked by tag icon next to them).

Fig. 7. Two concepts/tags added to one answer possibility

Fig. 8. Simple view with tags hidden when filling in a patient form.

4   Data Export

All trial-related data can still be exported in ontologically-enriched CDISC ODM as this format is currently still one of the de-facto standards for exchanging trial data. But in addition it is now further possible to export that data in the form of RDF either to a local file or by pushing it via SPARQL Update [6] to a connected triple-store. The overall structure of this RDF export is based on a newly defined vocabulary which is derived closely from the original CDISC ODM elements' specification re-using existing vocabularies, like the Dublin Core Metadata Set [4] as much as possible. The use of this "home-grown" vocabulary has the advantage that the resulting RDF (semantically) follows the original CDISC ODM very closely and is thus easily interpretable in this context but has the disadvantage of being non-standard. Therefore, in addition, an export based on the proposed FHIR RDF representation [12] is provided that integrates the approaches of both [5,7] for mapping CDISC ODM to FHIR.

5   Conclusions

As told above, applying ontologies in clinical trial management is nothing novel per se. The difference here lies in the strong focus on (1) ease-of-use which allows people without much (or any) "ontological background" to use ontologies and concepts in their regular clinical trial work approaches with little training through an intuitive and responsive user interface, (2) applying well established,

standard ontologies combined with current Semantic-Web technologies to foster both semantic and technical interoperability.
(Additional information can be found at https://purl.org/holger/monster).

References

1. Apache Software Foundation: Lucene. https://lucene.apache.org
2. Brochhausen, M., Weiler, G., Cocos, C., et al.: The ACGT master ontology on cancer - a new terminol. source for oncolog. Practice. In: Proceedings of IEEE Symposium on Computer-Based Medical Systems (2008)
3. CDISC Consortium: Operational Data Model (ODM). https://www.cdisc.org/odm
4. DCMI: Dublin Core Meta. Elem. Set. http://dublincore.org/documents/dces
5. Doods, J., Neuhaus, P., Dugas, M.: Converting ODM metadata to FHIR questionnaire resources. Stud. Health Technol. Inform. **228**, 456–460 (2016)
6. Gearon, P., et al.: SPARQL Update. https://www.w3.org/TR/sparql11-update
7. Leroux, H., Metke-Jimenez, A., Lawley, M.: ODM on FHIR: towards achieving semantic interoperability of clinical study data. In: Proceedings of SWAT4LS (2015)
8. National Cancer Institute: NCI Thesaurus. https://ncit.nci.nih.gov
9. Sanfilippo, E., Schwarz, U., Schneider, L.: The health data ontology trunk (HDOT) - towards an ontolog. represent. of cancer-related knowledge. In: Proceedings of IARWISOCI (2012)
10. SNOMED International: SNOMED CT. http://www.snomed.org/snomed-ct
11. Stenzhorn, H., Weiler, G., Brochhausen, M., Schera, F., Kritsotakis, V., et al.: The ObTiMA system - ontology-based managing of clinical trials. In: Proceedings of Medinfo (2010)
12. FHIR IS WG. FHIR RDF Representation. https://www.hl7.org/fhir/rdf.html

Variant-DB: A Tool for Efficiently Exploring Millions of Human Genetic Variants and Their Annotations

Joachim Kutzera[✉] and Patrick May

Genome Analysis, Bioinformatics Core, Luxembourg Centre for Systems Biomedicine, University of Luxembourg, Esch-sur-alzette, Luxembourg
joachim.kutzera@uni.lu

Abstract. Next Generation Sequencing (NGS) allows sequencing of a human genome within hours, enabling large scale applications such as sequencing the genome of each patient in a clinical study. Each individual human genome has about 3.5 Million genetic differences to the so called reference genome, the consensus genome of a healthy human. These differences, called variants, determine individual phenotypes, and certain variants are known to indicate disease predispositions. Finding associations from variant patterns and affected genes to these diseases requires combined analysis of variants from multiple individuals and hence, efficient solutions for accessing and filtering the variant data. We present Variant-DB, our in-house database solution that allows such efficient access to millions of variants from hundreds to thousands of individuals. Variant-DB stores individual variant genotypes and annotations. It features a REST-API and a web-based front-end for filtering variants based on annotations, individuals, families and studies. We explain Variant-DB and its front-end and demonstrate how the Variant-DB API can be included in data integration workflows.

1 Introduction

Genetic variants are differences in individual genomes to the reference genome, the generally accepted consensus genome of a healthy human [1]. Each individual human genome has on average 3.5 Million such variants, either homozygous or heterozygous [2]. Clinical cohort studies featuring Next Generation Sequencing (NGS) explore either the whole genome (WGS) or the whole exome (WES) for numerous individuals [2,3] resulting in thousands (WES) to millions (WGS) of variants per individual using standard variant calling pipelines like the GATK Best practice workflow[1]. These variants are typically stored in variant-call-format or vcf-files, which allow combining individual variant data for multiple individuals, variant calling quality scores and annotations per variant in one file [4].

---

[1] https://software.broadinstitute.org/gatk/best-practices.

© Springer International Publishing AG 2017
M. Da Silveira et al. (Eds.): DILS 2017, LNBI 10649, pp. 22–28, 2017.
https://doi.org/10.1007/978-3-319-69751-2_3

Variant annotations are properties of variants relating to their frequency in the general population, their location (e.g. protein- or non-coding genes, enhancer regions, etc.), their effect on genes, gene expression and, on a broader level, known phenotypes related to single variants or whole genes. Variants are annotated (enriched with such annotation information) using tools such as ANNOVAR [5]. Vcf-files with genotype and annotation information can be as large as tens of gigabytes, especially in multi-sample whole-genome analyses. While sequential processing of such files is possible using modern PC hardware, direct random access and filtering of such data is cumbersome.

To address that problem, several solutions for storing variants in databases have been developed, examples can be found in [6–9] or [10]. Each of these solutions has different features and focuses depending on their authors' requirements, and there is no universal turnkey solution. To meet our specific requirements, we developed the Variant-DataBase (Variant-DB) within the National Centre of Excellence in Research on Parkinson's Disease (NCER-PD). It stores both individual genotypes and variant annotations from numerous WGS and WES studies. In this short manuscript, we present Variant-DB and show how we can use its REST-API to connect it to translational medicine data workflows. We further show a use-case for the web front-end based on the publicly available PPMI dataset from the Michael J. Fox Foundation [11].

2   Methods

2.1   Implementation

Variant-DB was developed on a Intel Xeon server with 32 Cores and 380 GB of RAM. We use Debian Linux as operating system and PostgreSQL 9.6 as database server. The current database with about 35 million variants from thousands of samples uses about 100 GB on the hard drive. Variant-DB was also successfully deployed in a virtual machine environment with less CPU power and memory size.

The PostgreSQL database contains tables for individuals, genes, studies, individual variant genotypes and variant annotations, see Fig. 1 for a simplified database scheme. Each of the 25 chromosomes (1-22, X, Y, M) has its own set of two tables, one for the individual genotypes ("individuals-tables" in Fig. 1) and one for the annotations ("annotation-tables"). This allows access to all chromosomes in parallel for highly time efficient queries.

2.2   Data Import

Variant data in the Variant-DB is organized by study. All individuals are linked to a study and stored in a dedicated database table with name, disease status and other pedigree information. In future it will be possible to link more evaluated clinical data if available. Furthermore, each individual is linked to all variants for which genotype information exists. The variant data is imported

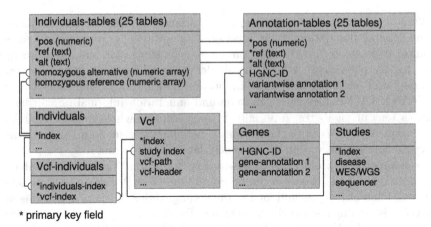

Fig. 1. Simplified table scheme for Variant-DB. Note that there is an individual-genotype- and an annotation table for each of the 22 autosomal chromosomes as well as chromosomes X,Y and M. The primary key of both tables consists of the same set of attributes (position, reference and alternative allele).

into Variant-DB from vcf- and gvcf files. Gvcf files additionally contain coverage information on the regions of the genome that showed no difference to the reference genome within a sequenced sample. We have developed python-based data tools for comfortable variant import and study management. Import operations are performed by these tools in a highly parallel fashion, processing all 25 human chromosomes simultaneously.

Annotation data for the variants is obtained using ANNOVAR [5] and other in-house resources, and converted into csv-tables before import. Variant-DB currently supports over 200 different annotation columns per variant and can handle data types such as text, numeric and array of text. Each annotation is represented by an individual field in the database. Hence, adding new annotations requires adding more fields to the variant annotation tables. Due to the separation between individual genotypes and annotations, this does not affect the genotype table.

Several modules of Variant-DB (import tools, server backend, web application) need consistent information about which annotations are supported. We store that information in a central text file (as tab-separated values) which is parsed by the different modules. New annotations are added to Variant-DB by adding rows to that annotation file and applying update-scripts that update the modules to support the new annotations.

2.3 Variant-DB API

We developed a dedicated representational state transfer application programming interface (REST-API) for Variant-DB for queries from web-applications. The API supports single-string commands sent via POST and GET requests and allows searching for studies, individuals, variants and other content. A typical search command for variants contains filters that limit the result to certain genes, individuals or annotation values. The query result then contains all variants in these genes that are present in any of the individuals at least heterozygous and that pass the annotation filters. A command can have an arbitrary number and ordering of these filters, allowing a highly customizable search. Short example API queries and their result are shown in Fig. 2.

The Variant-DB server backend is based on python and Django[2]. It processes the query command, determines the correct tables (e.g., for a gene-based variant search the correct chromosome tables that need to be queried) and creates the SQL-command that is then executed by the PostgreSQL database. The result data is processed by the backend and returned to the web application as JSON compatible data structure. Unlike classical JSON where each field is named, we use condensed JSON with only two key values: "fields" and "values". "Fields" contains the names of all columns in the returned data matrix, and "values" is a vector with a vector for each row that has an element for each of the named columns. Because JSON is submitted as string, this reduces the size of the response significantly, especially when the result table has thousands of rows.

We have developed a web-application as an entry point for exploring the data in Variant-DB, see Fig. 3. A variant search starts with selecting a study and individuals. Filters are available for chromosomes, genes, quality-scores and all variant annotations in the database. Several filters can be stacked in any user-defined order to specify the variant search precisely. The result is displayed as table in the browser, either summarized for each gene or with one row for each variant. The results can be displayed in the browser and downloaded as csv-file.

Query	Response of Variant-DB
`../individuals/getfields!eq!id,name&` `pedigree_phenotype!eq!2`	`{"fields": ["id","name"],` `"values": [[2,"PPMI_SI_3001_PD"],...]`
`../genes/getfields!eq!ensembl_gene_id,chrom&` `hgnc_approved_symbol!eq!tp53`	`{"fields": ["ensembl_gene_id","chrom"],` `"values": [["ENSG00000141510","17"]]}`
`../variants/getfields!eq!ref,alt,func_refgene&` `chrom!eq!12&start!eq!40651144`	`{"fields": ["alt","ref","func_refgene","chrom"],` `"values": [["C","T",["exonic"],"12"]]}`

Fig. 2. Example API-requests and the response from the database backend. Note that "!eq!" means "equals". We replaced operators such as "=",">" because these characters are not allowed in URLs.

3 Application Examples

The Parkinson's Progression Markers Initiative (PPMI) study is an effort to identify the biomarkers of PD progression. We use the publicly available WES data. Detailed information about this initiative and the data can be found on the

---

[2] https://www.djangoproject.com.

Fig. 3. The Variant-DB server webpage with filter-stack (shown left) and one of the filter selection pages.

website (www.ppmi-info.org/). Briefly, the variants were called following GATK best practices. The initial PPMI exome dataset contains 511905 variants. It is comprised of 404 PD cases and 183 healthy controls.

3.1 Exploring a PD Risk Variant in PPMI Using Variant-DB

The PPMI variants and their annotations were imported into Variant-DB. We selected all 587 individuals from the PPMI study. We then searched for the gene LRRK2 and in the annotation "aachange" (amino acid change) for the mutation "G2019S" which was previously described as a genetic risk factor in the context of Parkinson's Disease [12]. Searching all ca. 500000 variants takes one second. Only one variant passes the applied filter, and the result shows that the variant occurs in six affected and zero unaffected individuals.

3.2 Integrating Variant-DB with TranSMART and Minerva

Satagopam et al. recently described how big-data integration workflows can enable integrated analysis and visualization of (pre-)clinical and transcriptomic data [13] by linking the tranSMART, Galaxy and Minerva platforms. The Variant-DB described in this manuscript has also been integrated into the same workflow as source for genetic data in the form of variants. A scheme for the interaction between Variant-DB and the data workflow from [13] can be found in Fig. 4.

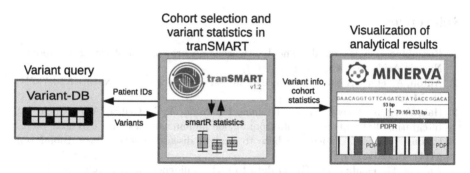

Fig. 4. Data flow between tranSMART [14] (http://transmartfoundation.org), Variant-DB and Minerva [15]. Users can build customized (sub-)cohort(s) in tranSMART by any clinical features. Then individuals in the cohort(s) are selected from tranS-MART and a request containing their IDs is sent to Variant-DB. Variants are returned to tranSMART, and summary statistics are computed by the tranSMART plugin smartR [16] (https://wiki.transmartfoundation.org/display/transmartwiki/SmartR). The results are visualized on the Parkinson's Disease map (PD-map [17]), which is based on the Minerva platform.

4   Conclusion

We have split the variant data into two tables for each chromosome for several reasons. Our setup allows the independent update, extension and versioning of annotations without altering the individual genotype tables. The separation of individual genotypes and annotations has the additional advantage that queries can be processed without the knowledge of any genotype reporting only the known annotation data for a given variant.

Variant-DB is work in progress. We have proved that our combination of PostgreSQL database and Django-backend is capable of searching millions of variants within seconds. Variant-DB is able to efficiently store and manage data from large-scale genetic studies and will in future be the main entry point of PD genetic data with the Luxembourgish NCER-PD program[3].

Acknowledgments. We would like to thank Dheeraj R. Bobbili for the help with the PPMI data, Marek Ostaszewski and Piotr Gawron for their support with the Minerva API, Venkata Satagopam, Wei Gu, Sascha Herzinger for their help with tranSMART. JK and PM were supported by the FNR NCER-PD grant. PM was supported by the JPND Courage-PD project. Data used in the preparation of this article were obtained from the Parkinson's Progression Markers Initiative (PPMI) database (www.ppmi-info.org/data) For up-to-date information on the study, visit www.ppmi-info.org. PPMI - a public-private partnership - is funded by the Michael J. Fox Foundation for Parkinson's Research and funding partners, including Abbvie, Avid, Biogen, Bristol-Myers Squibb, Covance, GE Healthcare, Genentech, GlaxoSmithKline, Lilly, Lundbeek, Merck, Meso Scale Discovery, Pfizer, Piramal, Roche, Servier, Teva, UCB, and Golub Capital.

---

[3] http://parkinson.lu/index.php/en/en-why-research/what-is-ncer-pd.

References

1. Rosenbloom, K.R., et al.: The UCSC genome browser database: 2015 update. Nucleic Acids Res. **43**, 670–681 (2014)
2. Auton, A., et al.: A global reference for human genetic variation. Nature **526**(7571), 68–74 (2015)
3. Hakenberg, J., Cheng, W.Y., Thomas, P., Wang, Y.C., Uzilov, A.V., Chen, R.: Integrating 400 million variants from 80,000 human samples with extensive annotations: towards a knowledge base to analyze disease cohorts. BMC Bioinform. **17**(1), 24 (2016)
4. Auwera, G., et al.: From FastQ data to high confidence variant calls: the genome analysis toolkit best practices pipeline, vol. 11 (2014)
5. Wang, K., Li, M., Hakonarson, H.: Annovar: functional annotation of genetic variants from high-throughput sequencing data. Nucleic Acids Res. **38**(16), e164 (2010)
6. Cheng, W.Y., Hakenberg, J., Li, S.D., Chen, R.: DIVAS: a centralized genetic variant repository representing 150 000 individuals from multiple disease cohorts. Bioinformatics **32**(1), 151–153 (2015)
7. Fokkema, I.F.A.C., Taschner, P.E.M., Schaafsma, G.C.P., Celli, J., Laros, J.F.J., den Dunnen, J.T.: LOVD v. 2.0: the next generation in gene variant databases. Hum. Mutat. **32**(5), 557–563 (2011)
8. MacDonald, J.R., Ziman, R., Yuen, R.K.C., Feuk, L., Scherer, S.W.: The database of genomic variants: a curated collection of structural variation in the human genome. Nucleic Acids Res. **42**(D1), 986–992 (2014)
9. Higasa, K., et al.: Human genetic variation database, a reference database of genetic variations in the japanese population. J. Hum. Genet. **61**(6), 547–553 (2016)
10. Vandeweyer, G., et al.: Detection and interpretation of genomic structural variation in health and disease. Expert Rev. Mol. Diagn. **13**(1), 61–82 (2013)
11. Steger, M., et al.: Phosphoproteomics reveals that Parkinson's disease kinase LRRK2 regulates a subset of Rab GTPases. eLife 5, pp. 1–28 (2016)
12. Bonifati, V.: Parkinson's disease: the LRRK2-G2019S mutation: opening a novel era in parkinson's disease genetics. Eur. J. Hum. Genet. **14**(10), 1061–1062 (2006)
13. Satagopam, V., et al.: Integration and visualization of translational medicine data for better understanding of human diseases. Big Data **4**(2), 97–108 (2016)
14. Athey, B.D., Braxenthaler, M., Haas, M., Guo, Y., Arbor, A., Alliance, P.: TranSMART: an open source and community-driven informatics and data sharing platform for clinical and translational research. AMIA summits on translational science proceedings, pp. 6–8 (2013)
15. Gawron, P., et al.: MINERVA—a platform for visualization and curation of molecular interaction networks. Nat. Publishing Group **2**(June), 1–6 (2016)
16. Herzinger, S., Gu, W., Satagopam, V., Eifes, S., Rege, K., Barbosa-Silva, A., Schneider, R.: SmartR: an open-source platform for interactive visual analytics for translational research data. Bioinformatics **33**(14), 2229–2231 (2017)
17. Fujita, K.A., et al.: Integrating pathways of parkinson's disease in a molecular interaction map. Mol. Neurobiol. **49**(1), 88–102 (2014)

Semantic Interoperability of Clinical Data

Jacqueline Midlej do Espírito Santo$^{(\boxtimes)}$ and Claudia Bauzer Medeiros

Institute of Computing, University of Campinas - UNICAMP, BRA, Campinas, Brazil
{jacqueline.santo,cmbm}@ic.unicamp.br

Abstract. The interoperability of clinical information systems is particularly complicated due to the use of outdated technologies and the absence of consensus about standards. The literature applies standard-based approaches to achieve clinical data interoperability, but many systems do not adopt any standard, requiring a full redesigning process. Instead, we propose a generic computational approach that combines a hierarchical organization of mediator schemas to support the interoperability across distinct data sources. Second, our work takes advantage of knowledge bases to be linked to clinical data, and exploit these semantic linkages via queries. The paper shows case studies to validate our proposal.

Keywords: Semantic interoperability · Mediator · Terminology · Ontology

1 Introduction

The ability to exchange data among computational systems is called *data interoperability* [1]. Systems (and data) interoperability has been studied for decades, but there is still much to be done. In medical information systems, one of the most adopted solutions is the use of data exchange standards. However, the constant appearance of new devices and collection methods has exponentially increased the data heterogeneity problem. This paper addresses the problem of clinical data interoperability. Besides technical issues, clinical data interoperability is moreover hampered by ethical and security issues, by the absence of consensus about standards and terminology, and by the use of outdated and closed technology.

In the healthcare context, the two main approaches to clinical data interoperability are: (1) Electronic Health Records (EHR) standards to model clinical information and (2) terminologies to establish common understanding of vocabulary and concepts. EHR standards define protocols to digitally store and exchange patients' health data. The most frequently adopted standards are HL7[1], openEHR[2] and ISO/EN 13606[3]. However, many systems do not apply

---

[1] Health Level Seven. www.hl7.org.
[2] OpenEHR Specification. www.openehr.org.
[3] ISO/EN 13606 standard. www.iso.org or www.en13606.org.

© Springer International Publishing AG 2017
M. Da Silveira et al. (Eds.): DILS 2017, LNBI 10649, pp. 29–37, 2017.
https://doi.org/10.1007/978-3-319-69751-2_4

any standard - they have progressively adapted introduction of new technologies and would have to be completely redesigned to comply with standards.

Research on the second approach (2) investigates the use of knowledge bases such as terminologies and domain ontologies. *Terminology* denotes all types of vocabularies, such as controlled vocabularies, thesaurus, code systems and so on. In clinical information systems, a terminology is used only to define a common understanding in the interoperability process, but does not explore any the semantics. The latter are achieved by use of ontologies to integrate several knowledge bases.

This paper presents a methodology for enabling the interoperability of arbitrary clinical information systems, exploring semantic aspects from knowledge bases instead of standards. As will be seen, this allows posing queries to data from arbitrary health centers, and also constructing new kinds of queries. Semantic interoperability allows relating facts that are not directly related, and knowledge discovery. Our proposal is backed up by a case study.

Section 2 presents the state-of-the-art on clinical data interoperability. Section 3 presents our approach. Section 4 shows two case studies using real data. Section 5 briefly presents initial prototype to query clinical data from distributed systems. Section 6 presents conclusions and future work.

2   Related Work

Table 1 summarizes some of the main research efforts on interoperability among clinical information systems. Column 2 indicates the interoperability strategy adopted. Columns 3-4 indicate which EHR standard is adopted, and expansibility options. Column 5 indicates whether medical terminologies are used.

Almost half of the reviewed papers uses a single EHR standard across many computer systems ([6–8,10]). Sometimes, the authors provide expansion to other standards ([7,8]). For instance, the Taiwan Electronic Medical Record Template (TMT)[7] can be transformed into HL7. Also, Li et al. [8] present rules to convert MML[4] versions and MML into HL7 to provide data exchange across countries.

The use of data standards may not be enough when systems are distributed and do not have the same data model. The mediator architecture is a classic strategy for interoperability of systems based on different data models. This approach defines a global mediator database schema and mappings between the mediator and local schemas. For example, Sartipi and Dehmoobad [12] propose a standard-based guideline to semantic interoperability in health subdomains, with HL7 to represent the information model in the clinical domain and the ACORD[5] standard for the insurance domain. The common part of the domain models (basically, their "intersection") produces the mediator model. On the other side, Azami et al. [2] do not define a single schema, but rather a set of hierarchical mediator schema to integrate health subdomains.

---

[4] Medical Markup Language. www.medxml.net/E_mml30/mmlv3_E_index.htm.

[5] Association for Cooperative Operations Research and Development. www.acord.org.

Table 1. Related work

	Interoperability strategy	Semantics		Terminology
		EHR standards		
		Standard	Expansible	
Jian [7]	Single standard	TMT	Transformable into HL7	No
Li [8]	Single standard	MML	To HL7. Other mappings can be made by user	Yes
Müller [10]	Single standard	HL7	No	No
Hosseini [6]	Single standard	HL7	No	Yes
Sartipi [12]	Mediator schema	HL7 + ACORD	Generic standard-based guideline	Yes
Azami [2]	Mediator schema	any	Generic: non-standard-based	Yes
Costa [4]	Mediator ontology	ISO/EN 13606 + openEHR	To standards based on dual-model architecture	No
Berges [3]	Mediator ontology	any	Generic: any data model	Yes
Dogac [5]	P2P + mediator ontology	HL7 + ISO/EN 13606	Generic: any ontology model	No

Berges et al. [3] and Costa et al. [4] also define a mediator model, but use the ontological representation of the data models. Costa et al. [4] define a common ontology for EHR standards based on a dual-model architecture (e.g., ISO/EN 13606 and openEHR). Berges et al. [3] use a generic approach independent from any standard. Local ontologies are semi-automatically generated from local repositories and are specializations of the common ontology.

Another approach is shown by Dogac et al. [5], who use Peer-to-Peer (P2P) architectures combined with a mediator architecture to create an ontological representation for each peer. It is a standard-based approach in which HL7 and ISO/EN 13606 are used to add meaning to the exchange process.

Besides the structural model, EHR standards define semantics for clinical information via conceptual model (e.g., archetypes defined in openEHR). The use of knowledge bases is another way to obtain semantics. In general, authors only use medical terminologies to define a common vocabulary. For example, Sartipi and Dehmoobad [12] propose a shared terminology system to add semantics to exchanged messages. A different application is to help the translation process, such as Li et al. [8]. However, unlike us, they do not use domain ontologies and do not explore the semantic relationships from these knowledge bases.

There are several integrated knowledge bases that can be explored in the health domain. For example, the UMLS[6] meta-thesaurus establishes links to 200 biomedical vocabularies. Also, the LODD [11] links data about drugs and the TMO [9] is a medical unified ontology. All these approaches model terminologies in an ontology language, allowing to link them to other domain ontologies.

3   Our Architecture for Semantic Interoperability

Figure 1 shows our architecture in two facets: (a) on the left side, a mediator-based structure for clinical data interoperability and (b) on the right side, semantic linkage with knowledge bases. These facets allow integrated access to clinical data, designing queries driven by clinical context and exploring semantics on query processing.

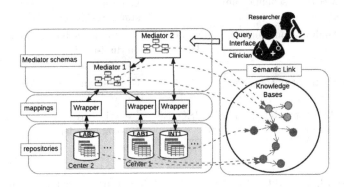

Fig. 1. Architecture overview

The left side is a hierarchical mediator architecture based on [2]. The bottom layer displays heterogeneous and distributed clinical data repositories from several health centers. We do not assume any standard about the center's data models. Ours is a generic and non-standard based proposal.

The mediator layer presents a hierarchy of mediator schemas to allow integration of subdomains of health information systems. The mediators at the lower levels define commons schemas to integrate each subdomain from all component health centers. In the figure, schemas from Center 1 and 2 are integrated in Mediator 1 (e.g., in laboratories). Other subdomains, such as Chemotherapy, can be integrated the same way. The mediators at the upper levels integrate the subdomains (using other intermediate mediators when needed)creating a global view of all repositories at the top of the hierarchy. The mediator schemas are designed in collaboration with domain experts.

---

[6] Unified Medical Language System. www.nlm.nih.gov/research/umls/.

The mappings layer stores the relationships between a mediator schema and those of individual repositories. For each local model, a wrapper sets the matching with the mediator schema, identifying sameness regardless of the structural and syntactic differences. Semantic links to knowledge bases can help find these correspondences between schemas, identifying different attributes linked to equivalent and/or even related terms. However, the repositories can have attributes that are not mapped. Usually, a mediator has a more global view that cannot cover all details. Also, more than one global mediator can be defined for different query purposes, e.g. clinical or research. So, besides the most common queries that are centered on a single patient, we foresee to query for sets of patients with similar symptoms Sect. 4.1 exemplifies the latter by setting the context by specifying results of tests, diagnostics, medications, etc.

This first facet allows users to recover data from different healthcare centers in the following way: (1) Users state queries based on the mediator schema; (2) Queries are addressed to intermediate mediator schemas and are reformulated according to mapping rules encapsulated in wrappers, creating subqueries consistent with the local schemas; (3) Subqueries are forwarded to the local models, which return the results back to the wrapper; (4) Wrappers unify the results according to the mediator schemas; (5) At the end, the results from all repositories are returned to the user interface.

The main difference between our proposal and standard mediator architectures is the possibility of queries using semantic links across clinical data sources and integrated knowledge bases (such as LODD [11] and TMO [9]). This second facet, on the right side of Fig. 1, considers links to knowledge bases from instances and attribute labels of the schemas. Various types of relationships can be exploited, e.g.: equivalence, composition, source, or causality. They can also be extracted from the existing relationships in the repositories. These semantic relationships can be exploited in query expansions - see Sect. 4.2.

4   Case Study

4.1   Interoperability of Laboratory Test Results

Let us now exemplify the mediator approach on real data from *Hospital das Clínicas*(HC) and *Hemocentro* databases at University of Campinas. HC is one of the biggest hospitals in Brazil, with 44 medical specialties and 5 thousand tests and exams performed per day. Its clinical and administrative information is distributed over 19 systems and many different DBMS. Hemocentro is a hemopathy specialized center, having a single information system.

Parts A and B of Fig. 2 show an excerpt of the schemas that define how results of laboratory tests are stored in each center. Part C presents a possible mediator schema, in which arrows show correspondences among the models. This example shows how lab tests are treated differently in Hemocentro and HC. E.g., result in the mediator schema is mapped to five attributes in HC schema. Also, attribute test_group in Hemocentro plays the same semantic role as the relationships between test and analysis in HC.

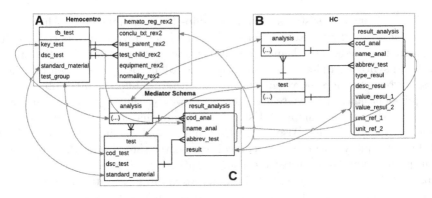

Fig. 2. Schemas of test results

Consider now **Query1** for *Platelet Count* (an analysis of *Blood Cell Count*) submitted to the mediator. Following the arrows, wrappers formulate **Query2** and **Query3**, addressed to Hemocentro and HC schemas, respectively. After these queries are executed, the results is unified and send back to the user.

```
        Query1                         Query2                              Query3
SELECT result              SELECT A.conclu_txt_rex2        SELECT desc_resul, value_resul_1,
FROM result_analysis       FROM hemato_reg_rex2 as A,      unit_ref_1, value_resul_2,
WHERE name_anal='Platelet  tb_test as B                    unit_ref_2
Count';                    WHERE A.test_child_rex2=B.key_test  FROM result_analysis
                           AND B.dsc test='Platelet Count';  WHERE name_anal='Platelet Count';
```

4.2 Semantic Enrichment in Querying Blood Cell Disorders

This section shows queries exploring knowledge provided by terminologies and ontologies in three ways: (1) **Synonyms**: to search a concept expanding the search to all synonymous terms; (2) **Generic concepts**: to search a broader concept, also recovering results from the specific terms; (3) **Relationships**: to search a concept that has a specific relationship with another concept. Part A of Fig. 3 illustrates a cut of the terminology SNOMED CT. It is the bigger clinical terminology - the US edition[7] in 2015 has more than 300 thousand unique concepts and 900 thousand relationships between concepts. Part B shows hypothetical records about the diagnosis of four patients linked to SNOMED CT.

To exemplify way (1), SNOMED CT lists synonyms for each concept. The figure shows the synonyms for Hb SS disease. Any term listed can be used to retrieve patients who have this disease. For example, when querying patients who have Sickle cell anemia the result would be Bruno.

To exemplify way (2), the arrows show is_a relationships. A query using a more generic term can return results from all its more specific terms by inference. For example, the query for patients who have some red blood cell disorder returns all patients, while the query for patients who have some hereditary red blood disorder returns André and Bruno.

---

[7] Systematized Nomenclature of Medicine Clinical Terms. www.nlm.nih.gov/research/umls/sourcereleasedocs/current/SNOMEDCT_US/index.html.

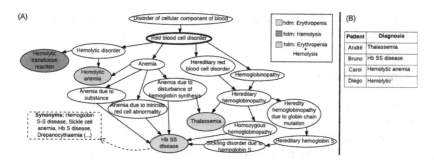

Fig. 3. Cut of SNOMED CT

To exemplify way (3), SNOMED CT defines other relationships via attributes. The colors show values given to attribute has_definitional_ manifestation (hdm): Erythropenia and Hemolysis. According to SNOMED CT, hdm "links disorders to the manifestations (observations) that define them". Erythropenia means the number reduction of red cells and Hemolysis means the premature destruction of red cells. A search for patients who has Erythropenia returns Carol and Diego. A query for patients with Hemolysis returns André, Bruno and Carol.

The combination of semantics and the mediator architecture allows expanding queries at each component center, thus providing a wide range of possibilities for research and treatment.

5   Prototype

Figure 4 shows a screen copy of first version of the prototype (in Portuguese) to perform clinical data interoperability among three databases: laboratory tests at Hemocentro and HC, and hospitalization at HC. This version is not yet semantically linked to knowledge bases. The left side is an interface to design queries,

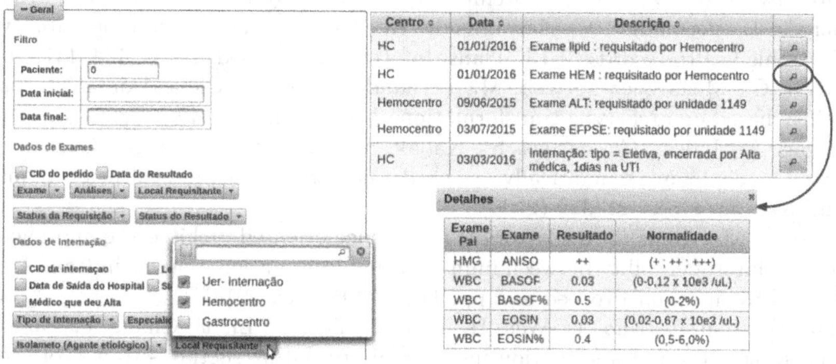

Fig. 4. Prototype interface

filtering by attributes. It allows users to specify the health context of interest. The right side shows results of a patient's medical history.

6 Conclusions and Ongoing Work

The paper proposes a framework to achieve semantic interoperability of clinical data in health information systems. We introduce a non-standard approach composed of two steps: (1) clinical data interoperability and (2) semantic enrichment. The first step uses a hierarchy of mediators to integrate distributed systems from different healthcare centers. The first case study exemplifies this step using real schemas from Unicamp healthcare complex. However, this example still faces problems about the use of different vocabularies, solved by semantic linkage.

This linkage brings new ways to explore clinical data, helping knowledge discovery. The second case study unifies the vocabulary and presents queries using SNOMED CT. Although most health centers use International Classification Disease (ICD) codes, it does not set semantic relationships between concepts.

Future work includes the expansion of the clinical subdomains, covering most computer systems at HC and Hemocentro. Our main effort is to establish links to integrated life science terminologies and ontologies and to explore this knowledge. Another promising direction involves ontology/terminology evolution, which will require dynamically refreshing system links and information.

Acknowledgements. Work partially financed by 1504650 (CAPES), 142243/2017-5 (CNPq), FAPESP/ Cepid in Computational Engineering and Sciences (2013/ 08293-7), INCT in Web Science. Our thanks to Hemocentro and HC collaborators, mainly Edson Kitaka, Profs. Fernando Costa and Erich de Paula.

References

1. IEEE standard computer dictionary: a compilation of IEEE standard computer glossaries. IEEE Std 610, pp. 1–217 (Jan 1991)
2. Azami, I., Malki, M., Tahon, C.: Integrating hospital information systems in healthcare institutions: a mediation architecture. J. Med. Syst. **36**(5), 3123–3134 (2012)
3. Berges, I., Bermudez, J., Illarramendi, A.: Toward semantic interoperability of electronic health records. IEEE Trans. Inf Technol. Biomed. **16**(3), 424–431 (2012)
4. Costa, C., Menárguez-Tortosa, M., Fernández-Breis, J.: Clinical data interoperability based on archetype transformation. J. Biomed. Info. **44**(5), 869–880 (2011)
5. Dogac, A., Laleci, G., Kirbas, S., Kabak, Y., Sinir, S., Yildiz, A., Gurcan, Y.: Artemis: deploying semantically enriched web services in the healthcare domain. Inf. Syst. **31**(4–5), 321–339 (2006)
6. Hosseini, M., Ahmadi, M., Dixon, B.: A service oriented architecture approach to achieve interoperability between immunization information systems in Iran. AMIA Annual Symposium Proceedings, pp. 1797–1805 (Nov 2014)
7. Jian, W., Hsu, C., Hao, T., Wen, H., Hsu, M., Lee, Y., Li, Y., Chang, P.: Building a portable data and information interoperability infrastructure - framework for a standard taiwan electronic medical record template. Comput. Methods Programs Biomed. **88**(2), 102–111 (2007)

8. Li, J., Zhou, T., Chu, J., Araki, K., Yoshihara, H.: Design and development of an international clinical data exchange system: the international layer function of the dolphin project. J. Am. Med. Info. Assoc. **18**(5), 683–689 (2011)

9. Luciano, J., Andersson, B., Batchelor, C., et al.: The translational medicine ontology and knowledge base: driving personalized medicine by bridging the gap between bench and bedside. J. Biomed. Semant. **2**(suppl 2), 1–21 (2011)

10. Müller, M.L., Ückert, F., Bürkle, T., Prokosch, H.U.: Cross-institutional data exchange using the clinical document architecture (CDA). Int. J. Med. Inform. **74**(2–4), 245–256 (2005)

11. Samwald, M., Jentzsch, A., Bouton, C., Kallesøe, C., Willighagen, E., Hajagos, J., Marshall, M., Prud'hommeaux, E., Hassanzadeh, O., Pichler, E., Stephens, S.: Linked open drug data for pharmaceutical research and development. J. Cheminform. **3**(1), 19 (2011)

12. Sartipi, K., Dehmoobad, A.: Cross-domain information and service interoperability. In: iWAS, pp. 25–32. ACM, New York (2008)

An Integrated Ontology-Based Approach for Patent Classification in Medical Engineering

Sandra Geisler[2]([⊠]), Christoph Quix[1,2], Rihan Hai[1], and Sanchit Alekh[1]

[1] Information Systems, RWTH Aachen University, Aachen, Germany
{Quix,Hai,Alekh}@dbis.rwth-aachen.de
[2] Fraunhofer Institute for Applied Information Technology FIT,
Sankt Augustin, Germany
Sandra.Geisler@fit.fraunhofer.de

Abstract. Medical engineering (ME) is an interdisciplinary domain with short innovation cycles. Usually, researchers from several fields cooperate in ME research projects. To support the identification of suitable partners for a project, we present an integrated approach for patent classification combining ideas from topic modeling, ontology modeling & matching, bibliometric analysis, and data integration. First evaluation results show that the use of semantic technologies in patent classification can indeed increase the quality of the results.

1 Introduction

One important factor for the success of research projects is the selection of project partners. Especially in interdisciplinary projects, the search for experts in unfamiliar domains is time consuming, cumbersome, and might not be as successful as expected. Hence, to assist the process of finding partners for a venture, a recommendation system is desired which speeds up the search and helps to discover collaboration opportunities. Medical engineering (ME) is a domain, in which usually researchers from several disciplines (e.g., biology, medicine, mechanical engineering, computer science) work jointly on a research project. Furthermore, ME is a highly innovative domain with short product cycles requiring a fast translation of research results into applicable products [7]. While on the one hand, a publication list of a researcher is a good possibility to create an author profile [16] with main research interests, a list of patents can characterize the ability of a researcher to translate research into exploitable results.

Patents contain a wealth of technical information used for the development of products, but are at the same time hard to analyze as they are written using special terminology and formulations [31]. As patent inventors are not only experts in their field, but also have a product-oriented view on ME research, they constitute interesting project partners. Therefore, we propose an approach which uses patent topic modeling, ontology mappings, and ontology matching to recommend collaboration opportunities.

© Springer International Publishing AG 2017
M. Da Silveira et al. (Eds.): DILS 2017, LNBI 10649, pp. 38–52, 2017.
https://doi.org/10.1007/978-3-319-69751-2_5

The mi-Mappa project[1] aims at finding suitable experts for ME projects based on patents and innovation fields. According to [20], an innovation field (also called competence field in the following) in ME is defined as an area which has significant innovation activity, future potential, and a value chain as complete as possible. The main innovation fields for ME comprise [9,20]: Imaging Techniques, Protheses and Implants, Medical Information Systems and Telemedicine, Interventional Devices, Systems, and Techniques, In-vitro Technology, Special Therapy and Diagnostic Systems, and cross-sectional topics, such as patient safety.

As pointed out earlier, product-oriented experts are especially of high value for a project in ME. Hence, experts, who are also patent inventors, are very interesting for our search. Therefore, we analyze patents and assign them to competence fields, if applicable, and implicitly also assigning the inventors of the patent to an innovation field. We do this assignment by following two different approaches. First, we do a topic modeling of the patents by clustering them into several topics. Subsequently, the topics are mapped to the innovation field ontology in which the innovation fields are described. In the remainder we will call this the *Topic Map (TM) Approach*. The second approach exploits the references to research publications in a patent. We analyze the classification terms of these publications and map them also to a competence field ontology. In the following we will call this the *Publication (PB) Approach*. By combining both approaches, we are able to assign a patent to a competence field and thereby building a profile of the inventor.

The paper is structured as follows. In the next section, we briefly review related work. Section 3 describes our integrated approach which combines the topic modeling approach and the referenced publication approach. We performed several experiments with our approach and compared multiple configuration options. The results of the evaluation are presented in Sect. 4.

2   Related Work

Patent analysis using ontologies has been applied especially for patent search [6]. The PatExpert system, for example, uses a network of ontologies and knowledge bases to enable patent search, classification, and clustering [27]. Trappey et al. propose a system that calculates the conditional probability that, given a specific text chunk is present in the document, the chunk is mapped to a specific concept of a given ontology [24]. Patent similarity is then based on the number of common matched concepts. This approach restricts the clustering to the terms of the ontology which might lead to missing important terms not present in the ontology.

Patent clustering and topic modeling are useful to get an overview of a set of patents. Tseng et al. propose a full-text patent clustering methodology which includes document clustering, term clustering, and multi-stage clustering to avoid skewed distribution among clusters [25]. Each cluster obtains a summary

---

[1] http://www.dbis.rwth-aachen.de/mi-Mappa.

title by statically calculating the most frequent terms in the clusters with correlation coefficient method. A bibliometric approach based on co-citation analysis is introduced in [15]. The co-cited documents are linked under the assumption that they share the subject matter. The result of the approach also indicates core competencies in the corresponding industrial field. However, using co-citations to group patents may lead to superficial results due to the lack of internal knowledge of the patents [30]. There exist various approaches for topic modeling [3]. Topic modeling assumes that each document can be created by first drawing a topic based on a probability distribution, and then for this topic drawing a word of this topic also based on a probability distribution [21]. The inversion of this approach tries to determine the best latent variables, i.e., the topics, on whose basis the documents have been created, also called *fitting a model* [21]. There exist different model representations, e.g., the Latent Dirichlet Allocation (LDA) [5] and the Correlated Topics Model (CTM) [4]. The LDA model uses the Dirichlet distribution to express the probability distributions for topics of a document and terms of a topic. It assumes the topics to be uncorrelated. The CTM instead assumes that the topics are correlated. For patents, topic modeling has also been used. For example Tang et al. use probabilistic topic modeling for patent analysis and mining [23].

Collaboration and expert recommender systems to find collaboration opportunities have been widely studied, and many proposed methodologies involve a manual process. For example, predefined criteria are analyzed, and scores are calculated and weighted based on these criteria [1]. For finding partners in supply chains, there have been already several approaches, using supervised and unsupervised learning, statistics, and analyzing criteria [28]. In the field of finding partners for R&D projects, no related semi-automatic or automatic approach could be found. Systems to find experts for a certain topic are based on self-disclosure (personal information maintained manually), authored documents, or social network activity [26]. The systems can also be categorized into expert profiling and expert finding [2]. The most recent works are using algorithms from social network analysis, such as the link analysis algorithms PageRank or HITS [18,26] and graph-based algorithms [19]. We will concentrate on expert finding using authored documents (e.g., patents & publications) as we do not need (yet) a complete profile of a researcher. Many document-based Expert Recommender Systems (ERS) are only using enterprise-level documents and are restricted to employees in the same company. In contrast, we propose a document-based approach which uses information from *any* publications and patents available. The DEMOIR approach [29] also utilizes ontologies and domain models for expert finding, but they use them to model the expertise and the domain and do not do any ontology matching.

In summary, all of the approaches may cover a part of our approach, but we present a novel approach which combines the use of patent analysis, clustering, ontology design, and ontology matching to recommend experts for a R&D collaboration.

3   Approach

We aim at assigning patents to competence fields by following two complementary approaches utilizing the semantics incorporated in the metadata of a patent and in the patents themselves. Regarding the metadata, we are especially interested in the publications cited in the patent as these provide additional information about the content and related content of the patent. The content of a patent is analyzed using text mining techniques and the creation of a topic map. An overview of the combined approach and the main components is presented in Fig. 1.

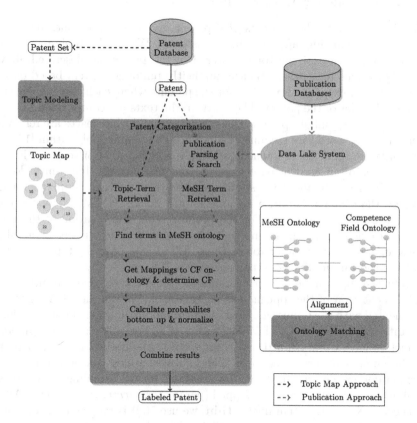

Fig. 1. Overall architecture of the combined approach (Color figure online)

The architecture of the approach consists of data sources, prepared intermediate results, and the main categorization procedure. The processing components are depicted in blue and green while the data sources and intermediate results are shown as yellow and white boxes, respectively. In the remainder of this section we will describe the architecture components and the workflow to assign a patent to a competence field.

3.1 Patent Database

For the analysis of patents, we need a comprehensive data basis with high data quality. In the course of the mi-Mappa project, a subset of the PATSTAT database (2016 Spring edition, version 5.07) published by the European Patent Office (EPO) is used. For our purposes, we selected patents issued by a German (DE) or British (UK) authority after 2004, which are from the medical domain (CPC class A61), and have an English abstract and title. This results in a set of 26814 patents. This patent set is the starting point for both approaches.

3.2 Topic Modeling & Topic Map

To analyze and rate the contents of a patent, we apply techniques from text mining, topic modeling, and document clustering. We build a topic map which gives us an overview of the topics covered in the patent set described above, and assign topics to a patent (hence, implicitly building clusters based on the topic). For this, we prepare a corpus for the patents where each text includes the title and abstract of the patent. The words in the texts are transformed to lower cases and special symbols, punctuations, numbers, and whitespaces are removed. Afterwards, the words are stemmed using Porter's stemming algorithm [17] and stop words are removed subsequently. We use a custom list of stop words containing terms often used in patents in the medical domain, but which do not have any information about the specific content (e.g., prevent, compar, prepar). Based on the cleaned corpus, a document term matrix (DTM) is created containing 27260 different terms. For the preprocessing and creation of the topic map we decided to use an R implementation as there are already many algorithms implemented. In order to create the DTM as a basis for topic modeling we utilize the tm and Snowball packages for R [14].

To fit the topic model in our case and to create a topic map, we utilize the R implementation of the topicmodels package [13]. We use the LDA algorithm implemented with the Gibbs sampling algorithm for estimation and a variational expectation maximization (VEM) algorithm [13]. For this algorithm, different parameters have to be defined, most importantly the desired number of topics and the number of terms per topic. The Gibbs sampling can be controlled by three parameters determining how the iterations for the sampling are done. An initial phase of iterations can be skipped (parameter *burnin*, we use 4000). Afterwards every X iteration (parameter **thin**, we use 500) is returned for a number of iterations (parameter *iter*, we use 2000). The draw with the best posterior likelihood of all iterations is returned in the end.

The resulting topic map with topics and their corresponding terms and the best topic for each patent and the corresponding probability (or multiple topics, if there are several topics with the same best probability) are stored in a relational database for later use in the categorization.

3.3   Publication Databases

Publications cited in a patent provide useful information about the content of the patent and we assume that they also contain information about the expertise of the inventors implicitly. It is common that patent inventors cite their own work to corroborate the knowledge they have about the described invention and cite related publications to delimit the invention from other work. Hence, we inspect the citations of each patent to gain further information about its content. The PATSTAT database contains also the references of the patents.

We then use one or more publication databases to search for the publications referenced in the patent and similar publications to retrieve more information about them. The databases should have a large number of publications in the domain of medical engineering, be queryable by using a web service, and having a classification scheme to categorize the publications. We analyzed several publication databases towards these requirements, amongst others Web of Science[2], European PubMed Central[3], OpenAire[4], and Scopus[5]. The only service which fulfilled our requirements completely was European PubMed Central (EPMC). It is a free publication database and provides full-text articles, abstracts, and further metadata. Especially interesting for us is the fact that many publications are tagged with terms from a controlled vocabulary, namely the MeSH (Medical Subject Heading) taxonomy. Therefore, we decided to use the EPMC database as a first data source for publication search. This can be complemented by other publication databases easily. We collect the MeSH terms from all publications found in EPMC for the patent to use them in a later step.

3.4   Data Lake System

We utilize our data lake system *Constance* [12] to store and query data from publication databases. It enables us to integrate data from different databases and at the same time use a unified query interfaces. As we are currently using only the EPMC database, there seems to be no need to use a data lake system. However, we are extending our data sources for patents and publications to have a larger data set for our approach.

3.5   Ontologies & Ontology Matching

Our approach is heavily based on the use of semantic knowledge. We want to detect and utilize the semantic knowledge which is present in patents as well as publications. Hence, we need a common, acknowledged, and comprehensive vocabulary which contains the knowledge. Especially for the medical domain, there exist several knowledge bases in form of ontologies and taxonomies.

---

[2] http://webofknowledge.com.
[3] https://europepmc.org.
[4] https://www.openaire.eu.
[5] http://www.elsevier.com/solutions/scopus.

We have to decide two things regarding the ontologies:

1. Which ontology can be used in its entirety to represent as much medical knowledge as possible. This will help to find the topics and categories of the knowledge represented in patents and publications in a structured and automatic way. As a corpus of patent texts can include a wide range of medical and non-medical terms it is more likely to find more of the terms in a broader medical ontology than in smaller specialized ontologies.
2. Which of the ontologies has the best coverage in terms of the competence fields? This will help to design a feasible competence field ontology (CFO) which is a subset of the selected ontologies.

We presented an analysis of medical ontologies due to their potential of representing the semantic knowledge for competence fields in [11] and will summarize our results briefly. The analysis shows that the most promising four ontologies are the National Cancer Institute Thesaurus (NCIT)[6], the Systematized Nomenclature of Medicine - Clinical Terms (SNOMEDCT) [7], Medical Subject Headings (MeSH)[8], and the Robert Hoehndorf Version of MeSH (RHMeSH)[9]. For these we did a coverage analysis where the coverage is the percentage of the innovation field terms (we used 174 terms extracted from [9, 20]) present in each of the ontologies. First we show that no ontology really outperforms the others and that the overall coverage is very low. Hence, we decided to analyze the coverage by adding one ontology after another, to see the gain of adding further ontologies. Starting off with the NCIT it can be noted, that we gain about 10% coverage using all ontologies. The biggest gain is achieved after adding the MeSH ontology. An analysis with the same terms using the Bioportal Recommender tool[10] delivered a similar result. Coming back to the questions raised above, the latter analysis and some restrictions led to the following answers:

1. We select the Robert Hoehndorf Version of MeSH as the overall ontology for semantic knowledge from the medical domain. The selection has several reasons. The first and most important reason is that we desire a MeSH ontology, because publications in the formerly selected publication database EPMC are tagged with MeSH classes. This helps us in finding concepts in the corresponding ontology easier. Second, the ontology is available as owl file. Other available MeSH representations are represented as rdf triples. The available format mainly consists of instances of general triple objects which are not easily usable for matching.
2. Based on the above results, we select the NCIT and the MeSH taxonomies as a basis for designing the competence field ontology (CFO) because they complement each other and offer the highest coverage.

---

[6] https://ncit.nci.nih.gov/ncitbrowser.
[7] http://www.snomed.org/snomed-ct.
[8] https://www.nlm.nih.gov/mesh.
[9] https://code.google.com/archive/p/pharmgkb-owl.
[10] http://bioportal.bioontology.org.

To reach our goal to map publication and topic terms to competence fields, we made a detailed requirements analysis including interviews with domain experts, analysis of existing ontologies, and an intensive literature research. Where applicable, we stuck to the NeOn methodology [22]. As described earlier we extracted a preliminary selection of 174 terms (the same terms as for ontology search), which corresponds to the sixth scenario "reusing, merging, and reengineering ontological resources" of the NeOn methodology. The terms have been used to make a first draft of a preliminary ontology which has been verified during expert interviews. Based on this and on the description of the competence field in [9,20] we completed the design and implementation of the ontology. The root elements of the ontology are the six competence fields. These are divided up in more fine-granular subconcepts.

Ontology Matching: To rate how strong a patent or publication is related to a certain competence field, we need to match the describing terms either extracted from publications or from the topic map to terms describing the competence fields. In preparation to this step, we create an alignment between the selected MeSH ontology and the competence field ontology. The alignment constitutes a set of mappings between the concepts of the two ontologies. This means, for each mapping we have a pair of concepts and a similarity value. To create such a mapping several approved and acknowledged tools exist. AgreementMaker [8] is an easy-to-use ontology matching tool and which achieved good results in the Ontology Alignment Evaluation Inititative (OAEI) challenges, also comprising a challenge with huge biomedical ontologies [10]. Hence, we used AgreementMaker to create an alignment between both ontologies. AgreementMaker is able to combine different matchers to create an alignment. We used the string matcher, the word matcher, the structural matcher, the lexical matcher, the cardinality filter, and the coherence filter. As a similarity threshold we used 0.6. The matchers have been combined in a hierarchical way and the default settings for each matcher have been used. The ontologies and the prepared alignment are stored permanently and are loaded at start up time of the patent categorization step.

3.6 Patent Categorization

The overall goal of the workflow for patent categorization is to determine for an individual patent to which competence field it belongs. The quality of this assignment is expressed by a score. In this section we will describe in detail the processing of the patent and how the competence field and the corresponding score are determined. The categorization process has been implemented as a Java application. The categorization procedure is in the beginning divided along the two approaches (Topic Map Approach and Publication Approach). Both approaches determine terms describing the content of the patent, but do this in different ways. After the determination of the terms the process works for both approaches similar.

Topic-Term Retrieval: The input of this step is a single patent. For each patent, the best topic (the topic with the highest probability) assigned to the patent is retrieved from the database. Each topic is described by a fixed number of terms which are also retrieved from the database. If there exist multiple best topics, each topic and its terms are processed individually. In the end the average over all topics per competence field is calculated to determine the overall score for the topic approach. For simplicity we will assume in the following, that we have only one best topic (the implementation allows of course multiple topics). The output of this step is a number of stemmed terms describing the topic.

Publication Parsing & Search: The input of this step is also a single patent. For the patents, all cited non-patent publications are retrieved from the PAT-STAT database. The cited publications are represented as one single bibliography string in the corresponding database attribute. Additionally, the quality of the publication representation also varies significantly, leading to inconsistent information retrieval from this string. Hence, we wrote a bibliography parser, which is able to detect the most important metadata elements (such as authors, title). Utilizing this information, for each cited publication, we search for the publications using our data lake system. Each search can deliver more than one result (not only exact matches are retrieved). For each returned publication the attached MeSH terms from the EPMC database are retrieved. From our experience, we were able to correctly parse and retrieve the tagged MeSH classes for only about 42% of the publications. If no MeSH classes are retrieved, no score is calculated for this approach and only the results from the topic mapping approach are considered. The output of this step is a set of all MeSH terms extracted from all cited and related non-patent publications.

Find Terms in MeSH Ontology: The input of this step are either the stemmed terms from the topic map or the MeSH terms from the publications. This step is separately executed for the two sets of terms. For each term we do a substring comparsion with all concepts in the MeSH ontology. If a MeSH term matches it is collected in a set. The output of this step is a set of MeSH concepts from the MeSH ontology.

Get Mappings Between MeSH Terms & CF Ontology: The input of this step is the set of MeSH concepts retrieved in the step before. For each approach a separate set of MeSH terms is processed. For each MeSH class in the set it is checked if

1. there exists a direct mapping, i.e., the mapping contains the MeSH class directly. In this case the similarity of this mapping is directly added to the confidence value of the corresponding competence field, or
2. an ancestor of the MeSH class in the MeSH ontology is contained in a mapping. Then the similarity divided by the length of the path is added to the confidence value for the corresponding competence field.

If a mapping is found, for the concept of the competence field ontology of the pair the root concept, i.e., the competence field is determined. To this competence field the above described calculated confidence value is accounted. Hence, for each of the found MeSH classes the corresponding confidence value is calculated. The calculation of the confidence value for the competence field k for concept c is presented in Eq. 1. i iterates over the N mappings found for M, sim_i is the similarity value for mapping i, and p is the path length to the mapped MeSH concept, where $p = 1$ for a direct mapping and $p > 1$ for a mapping to an ancestor is used.

$$\mathtt{conf}_k(c) = \frac{\sum_{i=1}^{N} \mathtt{sim}_i}{p} \qquad (1)$$

Calculate Scores Bottom up & Normalize: After the confidence value for each MeSH class and each competence field has been calculated, we do different calculations for the two approaches bottom up.

1. For the topic map approach we sum up the confidence values of all MeSH concepts found for each term of the best topic being involved in mappings. We calculate the average dividing the sum of all confidence values of all found MesH concepts with mappings by the overall number of found MeSH classes (no matter if involved in a mapping or not) per competence field. The calculation of the confidence value for term t and competence field k is presented in Eq. 2, where i iterates over M found MeSH concepts involved in a mapping, and C is the number of all found MeSH concepts for term t.

$$\mathtt{conf}_k(t) = \frac{\sum_{i=1}^{M} \mathtt{conf}_i}{C} \qquad (2)$$

Subsequently, the confidence value for a topic q and a competence field k is calculated by summing up the confidence values of all T termsand dividing it by T. Finally, we calculate the final confidence value for the patent p for each competence field k by summing up the confidence values for all Q topicsand dividing it by Q, if multiple best topics exist.
2. For the publication approach we sum up the confidence values of all MeSH concepts found for a term t as described in Eq. 2. Afterwards, the confidence value for a patent p and a competence field k is calculated by summing up all confidence values of all terms T per competence field and dividing the sum by T.

The output of this step are two sets (one for each approach) of six confidence values (one for each competence field). The scores obtained using the afore-mentioned steps are not uniform, owing to the variability of the depth of the competence field ontology for the different competence fields. Therefore, there is a need for normalizing these scores. After the score calculation step, we perform a normalization step, where each individual score is divided by the sum of all scores for that approach. The normalized scores for each of the approaches consequently adds up to 1, which gives us a much better representation of the relative confidence of the algorithm towards the different competence fields.

Combination of Results: In the final step of our system the independently calculated results from the two approaches are fused together to form a final list of competence fields. The *Amalgamation (AM) Approach* takes into account two factors, which are (i) whether or not both independent approaches agree on a particular competence field and (ii) the relative confidence with which each of the approaches reports a particular confidence field. Based on these factors, the two-step amalgamation algorithm is described as follows:

1. Determine the intersection of the two sets of maximal score competence fields returned by both approaches. Note that the intersection might be empty, if there are no common competence fields that both approaches agree upon.
2. Calculate the difference between the score values of the two competence fields with the highest and second-highest scores. Assign the top competence field from that approach which has the highest difference to second best competence field, i.e., we choose the top competence field from that approach which is more confident about the top result. Hence, the amalgamation approach makes sure, that the final result contains at least one competence field.

4   Evaluation

4.1   Measurements

In order to evaluate the accuracy of our proposed approach, we compute precision, recall, and F-measure for our results. Up to three competence fields can be assigned to a patent (by our approach and an expert). Therefore, we can compute these measures for each patent and then take the average for all patents in the test dataset. Although up to three competence fields can be assigned to a patent, most patents have only one, a few patents have two competence fields assigned by experts and by the approach.

4.2   Experiment Results

We report the accuracy of the competence field assignment results generated by the Topic Map and Publication approaches, as well as the Amalgamation Approach described in Sect. 3.6. We use a set of 20 patents which are randomly selected from the patent dataset mentioned in Sect. 3.1. All 20 patents have references to publications. The number of patents in the test dataset is low, as each patent has to be analyzed by human experts manually to get a ground truth. The set of 20 patents is the initial dataset to test our approach and to find the best configuration. A larger evaluation is planned with about 1800 patents and a larger group of experts.

For the Topic Map Approach we use nine different settings as shown in Table 1. For each setting, we use *tm_ntopics* to denote the number of topics, while *tm_nterms* stands for the number of terms applied for each topic. For example, in *ConfigA* we use 20 topics and 10 terms characterizing each topic. The choice of the configuration is based on the balance between accuracy and

Table 1. Settings of the topic map approach

ConfigA	tm_ntopics = 20 ; tm_nterms = 10
ConfigB	tm_ntopics = 20 ; tm_nterms = 25
ConfigC	tm_ntopics = 20 ; tm_nterms = 50
ConfigD	tm_ntopics =30 ; tm_nterms = 10
ConfigE	tm_ntopics = 30 ;tm_nterms = 25
ConfigF	tm_ntopics = 30 ; tm_nterms =50
ConfigG	tm_ntopics = 50 ; tm_nterms = 10
ConfigH	tm_ntopics = 50 ; tm_nterms = 25
ConfigI	tm_ntopics = 50 ; tm_nterms = 50

performance. For instance, we can select for the number of terms more than 50, but this leads to a higher processing time for the Topic Map Approach.

Figures 2, 3, and 4 depict the comparison of precision, recall, and F-measure, respectively, among the Publication Approach, the Topic Map Approach with nine different configurations, and the Amalgamation Approach. As we can see, the results from the individual approaches are less than 0.5 for all measures, whereas the Amalgamation Approach achieves more than 0.5.

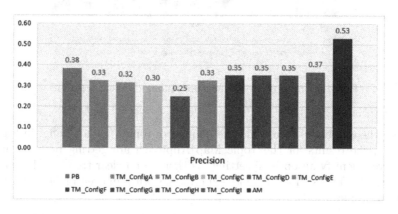

Fig. 2. Comparison of precision among different solutions

Still, this seems to be a relatively low percentage. The reason for this is that there exist certain patents for which the approaches cannot find cited publications in the publication databases, or the referenced publications do not contain any MeSH terms. If we are able to retrieve MeSH terms, the accuracy for the Publication Approach is more than 0.75. The Topic Map Approach still requires more fine tuning. A first analysis showed that the terms retrieved for the topics are too general and do not produce good matches with the MeSH ontology. If we

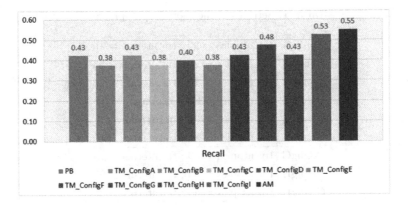

Fig. 3. Comparison of recall among different solutions

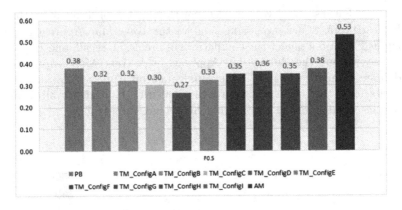

Fig. 4. Comparison of F-measure among different solutions

increase the number of terms and the number of topics (as in ConfigI in Figs. 2, 3 and 4), the results for the Topic Map Approach are getting better, but we cannot yet identify an optimal setting, as there is no clear trend in the quality of the results. This still needs more experiments with an even higher number of terms and topics.

5   Conclusion

We have shown an integrated approach to assign competence fields to patents in the domain of medical engineering. We described the competence fields in an ontology and used ontology matching to map the concepts of this ontology to terms retrieved using topic modeling and publication parsing. The first results show that using the cited publications of a patent is indeed a good hint to find the correct competence field. However, we are not yet able to find classification terms for all publications. Therefore, we will continue to work on our data lake system to make more classified publications available to our approach. The topic modeling approach still requires a more detailed analysis of the extracted terms for each topic. The results which we have so far show that there is a mismatch between the terms retrieved from the topics and the terms used in the ontology. Nevertheless, we think that our ontology-based approach shows the usefulness of semantic technologies in patent classification.

Acknowledgements. This work has been supported by the Klaus Tschira Stiftung gGmbH in the context of the mi-Mappa project (http://www.dbis.rwth-aachen.de/mi-Mappa/, project no. 00.263.2015). We thank our project partners from the Institute of Applied Medical Engineering at the Helmholtz Institute of RWTH Aachen University & Hospital, especially Dr. Robert Farkas, for the fruitful discussions about the approach and for providing the patent data.

References

1. Awasthi, A., Adetiloye, T., Crainic, T.G.: Collaboration partner selection for city logistics planning under municipal freight regulations. Appl. Math. Model. **40**(1), 510–525 (2016)
2. Balog, K., De Rijke, M.: Determining expert profiles (with an application to expert finding). IJCAI **7**, 2657–2662 (2007)
3. Blei, D.M.: Probabilistic topic models. Commun. ACM **55**(4), 77–84 (2012)
4. Blei, D.M., Lafferty, J.D.: A correlated topic model of science. Ann. Appl. Stat. **1**(1), 17–35 (2007)
5. Blei, D.M., Ng, A.Y., Jordan, M.I.: Latent dirichlet allocation. J. Mach. Learn. Res. **3**, 993–1022 (2003)
6. Bonino, D., Ciaramella, A., Corno, F.: Review of the state-of-the-art in patent information and forthcoming evolutions in intelligent patent informatics. World Patent Inf. **32**(1), 30–38 (2010)
7. BVMed. Branchenbericht Medizintechnologien, June 2015. www.bvmed.de/branchenbericht
8. Cruz, I.F., Antonelli, F.P., Stroe, C.: Agreementmaker: efficient matching for large real-world schemas and ontologies. PVLDB **2**(2), 1586–1589 (2009)
9. Deutsche Gesellschaft für Biomed. Technik im VDE. Empfehlungen zur Verbesserung der Innovationsrahmenbedingungen für Hochtechnologie-Medizin. Technical report, VDE (2012)
10. Faria, D., Pesquita, C., Santos, E., Cruz, I.F., Couto, F.M.: Agreement maker light results for oaei 2013. In: Proceedings of 8th International Conference on Ontology Matching, pp. 101–108. CEUR-WS.org (2013)
11. Geisler, S., Hai, R., Quix, C.: An ontology-based collaboration recommender system using patents. In: Proceedings of International Conference on Knowledge Engineering and Ontology Development, pp. 389–394 (2015)
12. Hai, R., Geisler, S., Quix, C.: Constance: an intelligent data lake system. In: Proceedings SIGMOD, pp. 2097–2100, San Francisco (2016)
13. Hornik, K., Grün, B.: Topicmodels: an r package for fitting topic models. J. Stat. Softw. **40**(13), 1–30 (2011)
14. Meyer, D., Hornik, K., Feinerer, I.: Text mining infrastructure in r. J. Stat. Softw. **25**(5), 1–54 (2008)

15. Mogee, M.E., Kolar, R.G.: Patent co-citation analysis of eli lilly & co. patents. Expert Opin. Ther. Pat. **9**(3), 291–305 (1999)
16. Portenoy, J., West, J.D.: Visualizing scholarly publications and citations to enhance author profiles. In: Proceedings of 26th International Conference on World Wide Web (WWW), pp. 1279–1282, Perth (2017)
17. Porter, M.F.: An algorithm for suffix stripping. Program **14**(3), 130–137 (1980)
18. Rafiei, M., Kardan, A.A.: A novel method for expert finding in online communities based on concept map and pagerank. Hum. Centric Comput. Inf. Sci. **5**(1), 1–18 (2015)
19. Rani, S.K., Raju, K.V.S.V.N., Kumari, V.V.: Expert finding system using latent effort ranking in academic social networks. Int. J. Inf. Technol. Comput. Sci. **2**, 21–27 (2015)
20. Schlötelburg, C., Weiß, C., Hahn, P., Becks, T., Mühlbacher, A.C.: Identifizierung von Innovationshürden in der Medizintechnik. Technical report, Bundesministeriums für Bildung und Forschung, October 2008
21. Steyvers, M., Griffiths, T.: Probabilistic topic models. In: Landauer, T.K., McNamara, D.S., Dennis, S., Kintsch, W. (eds.) Handbook of Latent Semantic Analysis, vol. 427, pp. 424–440. Lawrence Erlbaum Associates Inc. (2007)
22. Mari Carmen Suárez-Figueroa. NeOn Methodology for building ontology networks: specification, scheduling and reuse. PhD thesis, Univ. Politecnica de Madrid (2010)
23. Tang, J., Wang, B., Yang, Y., Hu, P., Zhao, Y., Yan, X., Gao, B., Huang, M., Xu, P., Li, W., et al.: Patentminer: topic-driven patent analysis and mining. In: Proceedings 18th ACM SIGKDD, pp. 1366–1374. ACM (2012)
24. Trappey, A.J.C., Trappey, C.V., Hsu, F.C., Hsiao, D.W.: A fuzzy ontological knowledge document clustering methodology. IEEE Trans. Syst. Man Cybern. Part B **39**(3), 806–814 (2009)
25. Tseng, Y.-H., Lin, C.-J., Lin, Y.-I.: Text mining techniques for patent analysis. Inf. Proces. Manag. **43**(5), 1216–1247 (2007)
26. Wang, G.A., Jiao, J., Abrahams, A.S., Fan, W., Zhang, Z.: Expertrank: a topic-aware expert finding algorithm for online knowledge communities. Decis. Support Syst. **54**(3), 1442–1451 (2013)
27. Wanner, L., et al.: Towards content-oriented patent document processing. World Patent Inf. **30**(1), 21–33 (2008)
28. Chong, W., Barnes, D.: A literature review of decision-making models and approaches for partner selection in agile supply chains. Purchasing Supply Manag. **17**(4), 256–274 (2011)
29. Yimam-Seid, D., Kobsa, A.: Expert-finding systems for organizations: problem and domain analysis and the demoir approach. J. Organ. Comput. Electron. Commer. **13**(1), 1–24 (2003)
30. Yoon, B., Park, Y.: A text-mining-based patent network: analytical tool for high-technology trend. J. High Technol. Manag. Res. **15**(1), 37–50 (2004)
31. Zhang, L., Li, L., Li, T.: Patent mining: a survey. ACM SIGKDD Explor. Newslett. **16**(2), 1–19 (2015)

A Conceptual Approach for Modelling Social Care Services: The INSPIRE Project

Elaheh Pourabbas$^{(\boxtimes)}$, Antonio D'Uffizi, and Fabrizio L. Ricci

National Research Council, Istituto di Analisi dei Sistemi
ed Informatica "Antonio Ruberti", Via dei Taurini 19, Rome, Italy
{elaheh.pourababs,antonio.duffizi,fabrizio.ricci}@iasi.cnr.it

Abstract. This paper proposes a conceptual model of social care services that takes into account different characteristics of services and activities. This model encompasses a multidimensional conceptualization of social and health care services integration, used in the Integrated Unique Access Point (IUAP), and considers those characteristics that are relevant to answer a fragile user's need. On the basis of the proposed model, this paper outlines the methodological considerations with regard to information management, modelling and design of data related to social care services. To this end, a taxonomy of services categorized according to different targets, i.e., elders and people with disabilities, is presented. Our model that is based on the UML standard is used within the INSPIRE project in order to achieve its required goals.

Keywords: Social services · Conceptual model · Taxonomy · Individual Care Plan

1 Introduction

Information and communication technologies (ICTs) play an important role in the contemporary society, where demands for social care services due to the increasing number of fragile people, especially elders and people with disabilities are growing. The adoption of these technologies facilitates, on one hand, to exchange information and share assessments with other professionals in the field of social work, and on the other hand, to convey, manipulate and store data related to social services. The importance of the use of ICT-based systems for the coordination and communication between social care professionals had been highlighted in the literature (e.g., [2,5,6,14]). Welfare systems are continuously under pressure to find innovative responses to demographic change, aging, etc. and for this reason these systems should tackle multiple challenges that confront social policy [13]. At European level, the recent efforts emphasize the importance of social innovation and technologies for improving the efficiency of social policies and their effectiveness in meeting societal needs, in particular in the context of social care systems. Thus, it is required to improve coordination and cooperation among social workers, by taking into account different needs of the

© Springer International Publishing AG 2017
M. Da Silveira et al. (Eds.): DILS 2017, LNBI 10649, pp. 53–66, 2017.
https://doi.org/10.1007/978-3-319-69751-2_6

target population (e.g. elders and people with disabilities). In this scenario, in order to achieve data integration, it is important to implement a common shared conceptual model that defines the concepts needed to facilitate sharing of both social care plans and their execution among different stackholders. This allows us to obtain continuity of social care from a business process point of view.

In general, the conceptual modelling has been acknowledged to be a powerful paradigm that enable us to receive better understanding of the problem under consideration and achieve a solution through a number of steps [12]. In general, the conceptual model refers to a conceptualization process, by which the problem domain can be represented by concepts and relationships at abstract level and serves to enhance the understanding of the problem complexity.

The main goal of this paper is to propose a conceptual model of social care services that takes into account different characteristics of services and activities. This model encompasses a multidimensional conceptualization of social and health care services integration that is used in the Integrated Unique Access Point (IUAP), and considers those characteristics that are relevant to answer a fragile user's need. On the basis of the proposed model, this paper outlines the methodological considerations with regard to information management, modelling and design of data related to social services. A taxonomy of services categorized according to different targets (fragile users) is presented. Our model that is based on the UML standard [1,4] is used within the INSPIRE (INnovative Services for fragile People In RomE) project in order to achieve its required goals. In particular, the INSPIRE Information System is defined on the basis of our proposed data model.

The paper is structured as follows. The next section provides an overview of the INSPIRE project, highlighting the system requirements in terms of different context applications, stakeholders and flows of data involved in various steps for defining the users' needs. Section 3 presents the conceptual model for social care services. Section 4 defines the taxonomy of services categorized according to different targets (elders and people with disabilities). Finally, Sect. 5 concludes.

2   The INSPIRE Project

INSPIRE (INnovative Services for fragile People In RomE) aims to contribute in reforming social care services, through an experimental pilot project in the area of Rome. It is important to underline that local governments (Municipalities) in Italy are responsible for care services especially for older and disabled people. There are fifteen municipalities in Rome, which are coordinated by the local government, namely Roma Capitale. The project focuses on the user and his/her needs and is conceived to be grounded on territorial synergies (public and private, professional and informal local resources). Thus, the main goal is to innovate and extend provided services and to enlarge the number of users so far excluded due to lack of economic resources. INSPIRE aims to launch the empirical test of a system of fragility care to be integrated with housing and employment policies, through training of social workers in local public bodies and in social cooperatives. It also makes social services an individual and community empowerment instrument. Social care services have been acknowledged as being key to face the emerging challenges in the European contemporary society, such as ageing or large female unemployment. This because they can timely react to households differentiated needs and to prevent phenomena of extreme poverty and vulnerability. Moreover, services diversification and integration seem to be fitting policy tools that are able to support vulnerable people and households in such economic crises as the current one. Nevertheless, in many European countries, like Italy, a reform of social services has been demanded for years, in order to obtain, on one hand, more spending efficiency - given that available resources are less and less - on the other hand a more personalized and integrated services offer. European institutions urge reforms evaluations to be evidence-based, in order to avoid further human and economic resources waste. To this end, the envisaged actions are: (i) mapping of innovative services for fragility care in the whole area of Roma Capitale, which aims to detect and collect all innovative interventions towards vulnerable people held in Rome; (ii) development of a District-based Operative Center, which aims to link the Unique Access Points (UAP) of local health authorities/municipalities and guarantee, from the client side, a fast access to the available services, and from the users side, the possibility of monitoring the fragile people; (iii) Realization of a shared and digital system for control and monitoring of fragile population, linking local general practitioners, local healthcare systems, home care services, and district guards. In this paper, we focus on point (ii), which relies on the development of the "reference access point" at district level in which different actors are involved, i.e., general practitioners, volunteers, neighbours, parish, etc. In this context, we study the information flow within the local authorities (i.e., municipalities) and design the underlying organizational model through a conceptual model, which is addressed to capture the main concepts and represent them in a comprehensive framework. The operative center is also linked with the UAP, as a strategic node to collect the different needs. Figure 1 shows the general schema for the mentioned District-based Operative Center, in which the different labelled paths are represented as follows: A - all the access points are connected via Internet to local autorities; B - The information system is connected to the local authorities as well as to local health centers in order to exchange informations, documents, medical record, etc.; C - the needy citizens interact with the operative center in order to apply their requests; D - the requests are gathered in the information system, which is connected to municipality/district, in order to be successively elaborated; E - the cooperatives/associations are involved in order to delivery the social services; F - The health centers as well as the cooperatives/associations provide services to the fragile citizens, and perform then the final assessment of delivered services and costs. Note that, in this project, particular attention has been paid on ethical and legal requirements in order to protect sensitive data in compliance with EU regulation on data protection [8]. The description of these issues is beyond the scope of this paper.

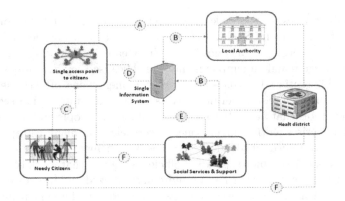

Fig. 1. The INSPIRE architecture

3   The Conceptual Model

In this section, the activity diagram and the class diagram are presented, while in the next section a taxonomy of social care services is given.

3.1   The Activity Diagram

In order to define the conceptual model for the INSPIRE project, the first step is to identify the main concepts to be considered for modelling the social care services provided to fragile citizens focusing the attention on the process point of view. It highlights the communication between different components at the semantic level by representing concisely the interactions between a subject of social care and social worker. In this perspective, the core of the system and therefore the main feature is *Individual Care Plan* (ICP) that is a plan tailored according to the social and health conditions of a citizen, which is considered for his/her social service delivery. Since the objective of the project is to provide an assistance based on integrated services, an ICP is described identifying the related main concepts as shown in Fig. 2. This diagram of activities describes the process followed by a case reported by a citizen to Integrated Unique Access Point (IUAP).

Based on the UML standard, the diagram is divided into three *swimlanes*, in each of which the activities of a particular actor of the system (in this case IUAP, Center of Complex Cases, and Competent Services) are represented (see Fig. 2). The initial node is placed within the swimlane that represents the activities of the IUAP, since the process begins when a citizen accesses to the IUAP. The first activity that takes place is a preliminary interview, in which the need expressed by the user is formulated. Then, the process can follow three alternative routes: (i) The need is purely social, and consequently, in this case it will be directed to the Social Secretariat; (ii) The need is purely medical; in this case the user will be addressed to the UAP of the Local Health Center; (iii) The need is both

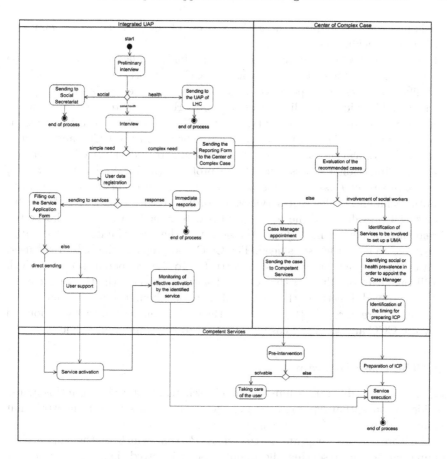

Fig. 2. The activity diagram of IUAP

social and health types, and consequently in order to better examine the need, an interview will be carried out. In this case we have two different alternatives described as follows:

1. As mentioned before, if the need of the user concerns both social and health care, then an interview with workers of municipality and local health center is carried out. In the case of a simple need, as a first step, the user data is registrated. Then, two options to elaborate the user request are considered, which are: an immediate response is provided to the user that results to end the process or the request will be sent to the competent services. In this last case, a form is filled out and the user is addressed to the appropriate services. At this point, the next activity, namely the *Service activation*, is placed in the swimlane regarding the competent services (i.e., Elderly Care Center, Disabled Adult Center, etc.), as it is an activity that does not directly concern the IUAP but the service/s addressed to fulfil the user request. After the completion of this activity, it returns to the swimlane of the IUAP, since

it is necessary to monitor the entire process of the activity, which may end after the checking phase.

2. In the case of a complex need, a reporting form is filled out in order to be sent to the Center of Complex Cases (CCC for short), where on the basis of different necessary experiences and competencies (i.e., social, health, etc.), the Social Services Coordinator of the Local Health Center, the Head of the Social Service of the municipality, and the Director of the Local Health Center are involved. At this point the activity begins in the CCC, and consists of: (i) Identification of services to be considered and the need to perform a multidimensional assessment of the problem (in Fig. 2 shown as *unit of multidimensional assessment-UMA*), because the need of the user refers to both social and health care services. According to this assessment, the health or social prevalence of the user's need is determined, in order to choose the reference person, namely *Case Manger*, who then coordinates the activities required to meet the user's need. The CCC also prepares the ICP of the user. After this last activity, the case is entrusted to the competent services which will take care of filling in the ICP and service delivery; (ii) the case can be simply solved directly in the CCC and therefore the multidimensional assessment is not required. In this situation, the Case Manager is directly appointed by the CCC and then the case is delivered to the competent services.

3.2   The Class Diagram

In Fig. 3 the class diagram is illustrated. The schema, that is shown in this figure, provides a conceptual representation of the whole social service framework that is composed by a set of the principal classes.

The core of this diagram is the class *Person*, which is the super class of three classes, representing the main persons involved, i.e., *Contact_person*, *Social_worker* and *Assisted_person*. The class *Contact_person* represents the reference figure of an organization and for this reason is associated with the class *Organization*. The class *Social_worker* in turn consists of two subclasses, which are *Municipal_socialworker* and *Organization_socialworker*, depending on where these figures operate; in fact, in the case of *Organization_socialworker* there is an association with the class *Organization*, while for *Municipal_socialworker* there is an association with the *Municipality* class, which precisely identifies in which municipality the social worker works. Finally, the *Assisted_person* class represents the citizen who has a social need and this class is characterized by attributes such as *user_code*, *access_type*, *education_level*, etc., and it is related to the class *Municipality* by a *belongs_to* relation. Furthermore, this class is related to the class *Household* in order to know, for the purpose of a service assignment, if the user belongs or not to a household, and if so such a family by how many components is composed of.

Obviously the assisted person requires a need, represented by the class *Assisted_need* that will be managed by the social worker through the assignment of a protocol (represented in the diagram by an association class, called *expose*) and will require the delivery of certain documents by the citizen, such as

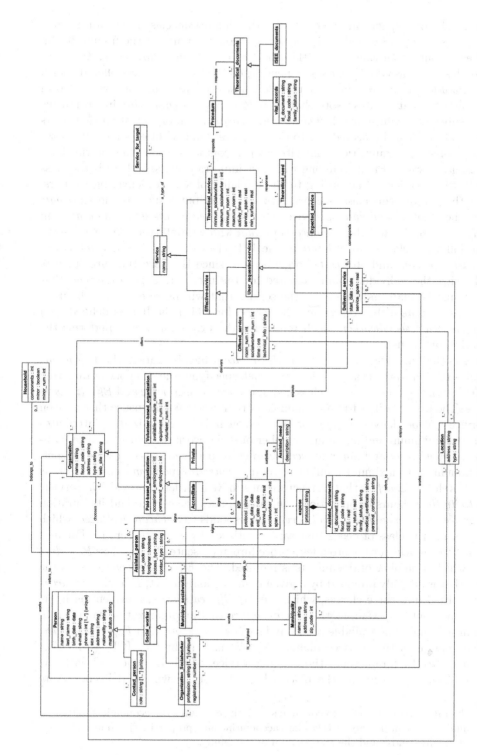

Fig. 3. The UML class diagram

the ISEE[1] or his/her family status. Another important class in this diagram is the class *Organization*, which is the service provider aimed at the fragile citizen. The attributes that characterize this class are, e.g., *name, address*, etc. As we can see, this class has two subclasses, depending on the type of services offered, which are *Paid-based_organization* and *Volunteer-based_organization*, each with its own characteristic attributes. Note that class *Paid-based_organization* in turn, owns two subclasses, which are *Accredited* and *Private*, as an organization that offers paid services can be accredited to one or more municipalities, or in the latter case, being an organization that citizens can contact without the intermediary of social workers. Finally, among the most important classes, there is the class ICP, which is defined according to the modality of service delivering to users. For this reason, this class is characterized by attributes such as the *start_date* and the eventual *end_date* of service delivery, the *planned_hours*, the *duration* in terms of months and the *socialworkers_num* who will intervene. As we observe the following classes are related to the ICP class: (i) *Municipal_socialworker, Assisted_person*, and *Accredited* organization, since they are the three players who sign the individual plan prepared for the user; (ii) *Expected_service* that contains the main indications of the service that will be reserved for the user; the *Assisted_need* that represents the reason for which the ICP is defined; (iii) *Organization_socialworker* which represents the professional who performs the service for the user.

Another important class is the class *Service*, which is characterized by *name*, and is related to the class *Service_for_target*, specifying the category of targeting fragile citizens. The service is classified into *Theoretical_service* and *Effective_service*. The first specifies the minimum condition necessary to ensure that a given service can be delivered, and for this reason it is characterized by attributes such as minimum and maximum number of social workers, represented by *minnum_socialworker* and *maxnum_socialworker*, respectively, who must be present, minimum and maximum number of rooms (*maxnum_room, minnum_room*), as well as the *min_surface* that a structure must have in order to provide the service, *activity_time* (hours of operation) which comprises the service and its duration (*service_span*). The *Theoretical_service* corresponds to a *Theoretical_need*, which represents the class of needs that can be satisfied by a generic service. Furthermore *Theoretical_service* provides a procedure, represented by the class *Procedure* for which a number of documents is required. The *Effective_service* class is the one that is actually provided by a given organization. In fact, *Effective_service* is specialized into three classes, which are: (i) *Offered_service*, representing information about, for example, the type of service that an organization can offer, in terms of number of available rooms and socialworkers, etc., (ii) *Expected_service*, that represents the services planned for the user in his/her ICP; (iii) *Delivered_service* that represents the ongoing service, which is associated with the class *Location*, specifying the place where the service will be delivered. Note

---

[1] The ISEE (Indicator of the economic situation) estimates the economic situation of families resident in Italy. It takes into account income, properties (i.e. houses, shares, assets, dividends) and the composition of the family.

that the *Service_target* class mentioned above has its own classification that is described in the next section.

4   Target of Services: A Taxonomy

As mentioned above the target of services form the core of the social services, and in order to capture the semantics of their peculiar characteristics a taxonomy framework is used. A taxonomy is a versatile system that can be applied in many fields, e.g., biology, living organisms, epidemiology, etc. [3,10]. In general, a taxonomy about terms or concepts (in our case, services) is a systematic classification according to a hierarchy that goes from the general concepts to more specific ones [9]. The taxonomy defined in this paper, which is based on the ISA hierarchy, is a tree-based structure that is defined by a root node and a set of nodes, representing the sub-categories. Note that the taxonomy that we present in this section is constructed on the basis of the Latium Region-Nomenclature of Social Services [11] (that is in line with the National Nomenclature [7]), in which a textual description for each service has been given. The analysis of these textual descriptions has led to identify several macro-categories, where each macro-category is further divided into homogeneous sub-categories with a lower level of generality and therefore more specific details. In this way a hierarchical classification articulated on various levels of detail is built, where the more specific categories have a higher degree of detail than the highest categories. This taxonomy is a part of the INSPIRE project aiming at organizing, in an orderly and comprehensive manner, the main characteristics of services so that the social workers can easily find the ones that better match the user needs. The social services by targets are classified according to Fig. 4. The main targets are elderly people, adults with disability, women in need, immigrants, etc.

In the INSPIRE project, as mentioned before, the targeted individuals are elders and adults with disability. This schema of targets is mapped onto the one of the social services shown in Fig. 5, where the general concept *Social Services* is classified into more specific concepts or classes, which are *Residential and Semi-residential Services, Care Services, Information and Consulting Services,*

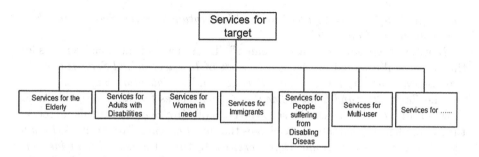

Fig. 4. Services for target

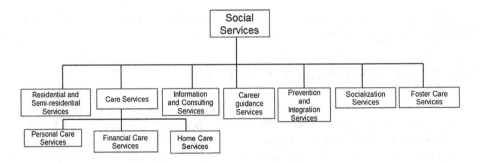

Fig. 5. Social services hierarchy

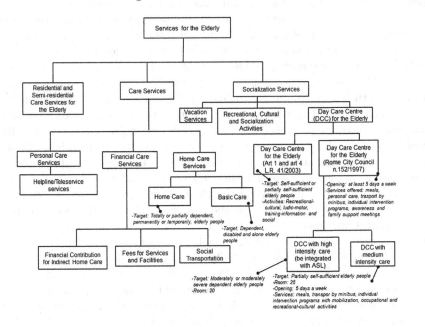

Fig. 6. Services for the elderly

Career guidance Services, Prevention and Integration Services, Socialization Services and *Foster Care Services.*

Now, let us consider the target "elders". The schema of the social services for this target is illustrated in Fig. 6. It consists of *Residential and Semi-residential Care Services for the Elderly, Care Services,* and *Socialization Services.*

The *Residential and Semi-residential Care Services for the Elderly* schema is shown in Fig. 7, while as can be seen the class of *Care Services* for this target, in turn, is further divided into three classes that are *Personal Care Services, Financial Care Services* and *Home Care Services.* In turn, the class *Financial Care Services* is classified into three subclasses that are *Financial Contribution for Indirect Home Care, Fees for Services and Facilities* and *Social Transportation.*

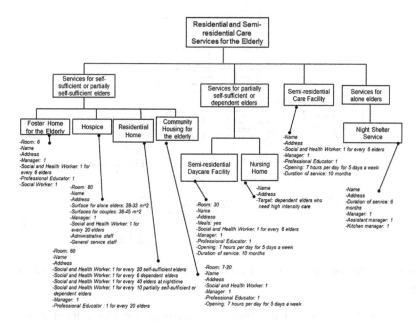

Fig. 7. Residential and Semi-residential Care Services for the Elderly

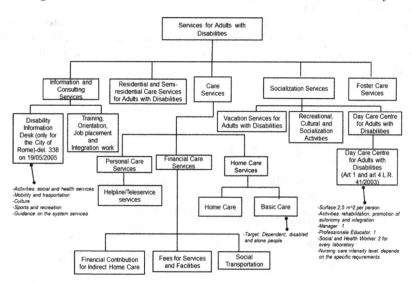

Fig. 8. Services for adults with disabilities

The class *Home Care Services* is divided into *Home Care* and *Basic Care*. Similarly, the class *Socialization Services* specializes in three sub-classes, which are *Vacation Services*, *Recreational, Cultural and Socialization Activities* and *Day Care Center (DCC) for the Elderly*.

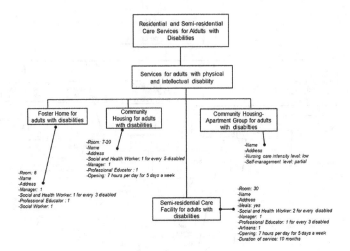

Fig. 9. Residential and Semi-residential Care Services for Adults with Disabilities

Similarly, Figs. 8 and 9 illustrate, respectively, the hierarchical structures of *Services for Adults with Disabilities* and *Residential and Semi-residential Services for Adults with Disabilities*.

The above mentioned classification schemes have been implemented by using the open source ontology building Protégé[2]. For the space limitation, only two schemes are shown in Figs. 10 and 11, where only a subset of attributes are visualized.

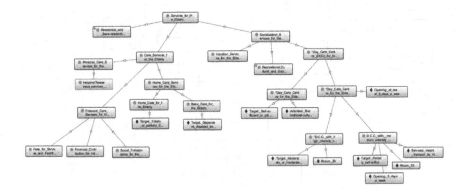

Fig. 10. Illustration of services for the elderly

---

[2] http://protege.stanford.edu/.

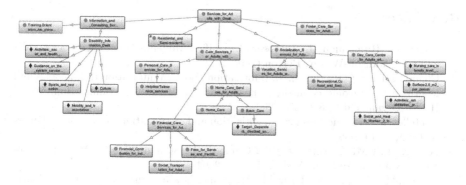

Fig. 11. Illustration of services for adults with disabilities

5 Conclusion

In this paper, we proposed a conceptual approach to model the social care services by taking into account various characteristics of services and activities. To this end, particular attention has bee paid to nomenclatures and standards for service delivery. The proposed model is based on the multidimensional conceptualization of social and health care services integration, focusing on the user needs. Note that the presented data model and taxonomy have been checked and validated by social workers of the *Department of Social Policies, Subsidiarity and Health Care* of Roma Capitale. As mentioned in Sect. 4, the taxonomy has been constructed on the basis of the Latium Region-Nomenclature of Social Services [11] that is in line with the National Nomenclature [7]. However, this taxonomy can be generalized to any kind of social care services by the support of a panel of international domain experts.

In the city of Rome there are various social communities, including a significant number of volunteers that offer services. The offers of these communities vary in terms of type, users and territorial areas served. Since in the city of Rome, the demand of social services is constantly increasing, these new forms of service offering should be better highlighted. In this direction, the taxonomy presented in this paper can be exploited in order to check quickly the compliance of the various offered services according to standard rules of service delivery.

Acknowledgment. The authors would like to thank Dott. Antonia Caruso, Dott. Daniela Lutri and Dott. Edoardo Trulli for providing us insightful information on IUAP in several interviews and joint discussions.

This study is part of the INSPIRE (Innovative Services for fragile People in Rome) project, EASI 2014 - PROGRESS AXIS - DG EMPLOYMENT AND SOCIAL INCLUSION, Grant Agreement n. VS/2015/0210.

References

1. Booch, G., Rumbaugh, J., Jacobson, I.: Unified Modelling Language User Guide, 2nd edn. Addison-Wesley, Boston (2005)
2. Chandrasekhar, C.P., Ghosh, J.: Information and communication technologies and health in low income countries: The potential and the constraints. Bull. World Health Organ. **79**(9), 850–855 (2001)
3. Centelles, M.: Taxonomies for categorization and organization in Web Sites. Hipertext.net, p. 3 (2005)
4. Fowler, M.: UML Distilled: A Brief Guide to the Standard Object Modeling Language, 3rd edn. Addison-Wesley, Boston (2004)
5. Merino, M., Marquès, M., Egurbide, M., Romo, M., Rodrguez, I., Garca, M., Ponce, S., Fullaondo, A., Mora, J., de Manuel, E.: Up-scaling of an integrated care model for frail elderly patients. Int. J. Integr. Care **16**(6), A251 (2016)
6. Perron, B.E., Taylor, H.O., Glass, J.E., Margerum-Leys, J.: Information and communication technologies in social work. Adv. Soc. Work **11**(2), 67–81 (2010)
7. Nomenclature of Interventions and Social Services (Nomenclatore degli Interventi e Servizi Sociali), Ministero del lavoro e delle Politiche Sociali. Conferenza delle Regioni e delle Province Autonome-CISIS, Version 2 (2013)
8. Regulation (EU) 2016/679 of the European Parliament and of the Council on the protection of natural persons with regard to the processing of personal data and on the free movement of such data, and repealing Directive 95/46/EC (2016)
9. Storey, V.C.: Understanding semantic relationships. VLDB J. **2**(4), 455–488 (1993)
10. Sujatha, R., Krishna Rao, B.R.: Taxonomy construction techniques - issues and challenges. Indian J. Comput. Sci. Eng. **2**(5), 661–671 (2011)
11. Taxonomy of Structures and Social Services of Latium (Tassonomia delle Strutture e dei Servizi Sociali del Lazio), Regione Lazio (2011)
12. York, A.S.: Towards a conceptual model of community social work. British J. Soc. Work **14**(1), 241–255 (1984)
13. Voigt, C., Misuraca, G., Lipparini, F.: ICT-enabled social innovations in social services. In: International Conference for E-Democracy and Open Government, pp. 105–114. IEEE Computer Society (2016)
14. Wong, Y.L.I., Solomon, P.L.: Community integration of persons with psychiatric disabilities in supportive independent housing: a conceptual model and methodological considerations. Mental Health Serv. Res. **4**(1), 13–28 (2002)

DyKOSMap: From a Research Prototype to a Web Application

Marwa Chaabane[1,2], Silvio Domingos Cardoso[1,3], Cédric Pruski[1(✉)],
and Marcos Da Silveira[1]

[1] LIST, Luxembourg Institute of Science and Technology,
5, Avenue des Hauts-Fourneaux, 4362 Esch-sur-Alzette, Luxembourg
{marwa.chaabane,silvio.cardos,cedric.pruski,marcos.dasilveira}@list.lu
[2] ReDCAD, Research Laboratory on Development and Control
of Distributed Applications, University of Sfax, Sfax, Tunisia
[3] LRI, University of Paris-Sud XI, Orsay, France

Abstract. DyKOSMap is a research prototype developed in the framework of the DynaMO project. It aims to maintain existing mappings established between knowledge organization systems (KOSs) by taking into account information about the dynamics of these KOSs. The aim of this work is to implement a Web application, in order to make a more robust and easier-to-manipulate tool starting from this prototype.

Keywords: DyKOSMap · Web application · Life sciences

1 Introduction

Knowledge Organization Systems (KOS) and their associated mappings play an important role in decision support systems. However, because of their highly dynamic nature, KOS entities are modified over time, impacting mappings and potentially turning them invalid.

In this context, DyKOSMap [1–3] is a research prototype developed in the framework of the DynaMO[1] project, in order to adapt these outdated mappings.

On the other hand, since it is a research prototype, DyKOSMap was still inappropriate to be used by non-ICT experts. Hence, the need to implement an interface to make an easier and more intuitive use of this prototype was needed to reach a broader community of users.

In this work, we start from DyKOSMap's prototype to implement a Web application using standards, Java language and following an MVC architecture. The paper is structured as follows. Section 2, introduces features provided by our application. Then, we present our conclusion and future work in Sect. 3.

---

[1] https://www.list.lu/en/research/itis/project/dynamo/.

© Springer International Publishing AG 2017
M. Da Silveira et al. (Eds.): DILS 2017, LNBI 10649, pp. 67–70, 2017.
https://doi.org/10.1007/978-3-319-69751-2_7

2   Provided Features

The operating principal of DyKOSMap is based on two main phases as depicted
in Fig. 1. The first one consists in maintaining automatically outdated mappings. The second one deals with the intervention of domain experts to validate
whether the output of the precedent phase is correct or not. To this end, we
defined two users' categories: *standard users*, this category includes knowledge
and data engineers and *expert users* which includes experts of the biomedical
domain whose intervention will be required during the mapping validation phase.
Concerning our Web application interface, we propose to divide mapping maintenance processing into successive steps and provide elements according to each
step as explained in Fig. 1.

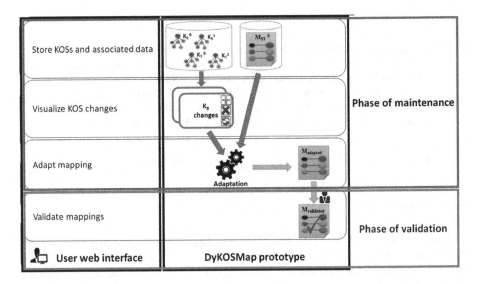

Fig. 1. The architecture of DyKOSMap Web application. This figure shows the relationship between the user interface layer and the processing layer (DyKOSMap prototype). Each feature provided in the interface calls for a specific step in mapping
maintenance process. K_S^0: KOS source at time $= i$, K_S^1: source at time $= i+1$, K_T^0:
KOS target at time $= i$, K_T^1: KOS source at time $= i+1$, K_{ST}^0 and $M_{adapted}$: adapted
mappings, $M_{validated}$: validated mappings.

Table 1 shows the main elements that our Web application interface provides
to each user according to his privileges. In the remainder of this section, we will
detail each element.

Once authenticated, the user can upload a new KOS or set of mappings as
an OWL file or by providing the appropriate URL. Figure 2 represents the Web
interface through which user can add new KOS to the system.

In addition, this interface allows visualizing the list of KOSs' stored is the
system or search for a specific KOS, getting information about each stored KOS

Table 1. Application's features

Features	Description	Required privileges
Registration Connection Profile edition	The user needs to create an account to use the application. Through which, the user can connect/disconnect to/from the application. Users have the possibility to modify his profile preferences	none
KOSs and mappings storage	The user can import KOSs and associated mappings in his dedicated database	none
KOS changes computation and visualization	The user can compute and visualize statistics about changes in different versions of KOSs stored in his database	none
Mappings adaptation	The user can ask the system to maintain outdated mappings, which are stored in his database, according to KOS changes	none
Mappings validation	The user is allowed to access all the adapted mappings already maintained by each user in order to validate it	expert

and removing a specific KOS. A similar web interface is provided to allow user to manage his mappings's database. Furthermore, we propose another interface to compute and visualize changes between two KOS versions already stored. Store KOS interface, store mappings interface and compute and visualize KOS changes interface are mandatory to set required outputs for the adaptation step.

The adaptation interface allows to select the appropriate inputs to get an adapted mapping as output. Yet, the obtained adapted mapping may contain

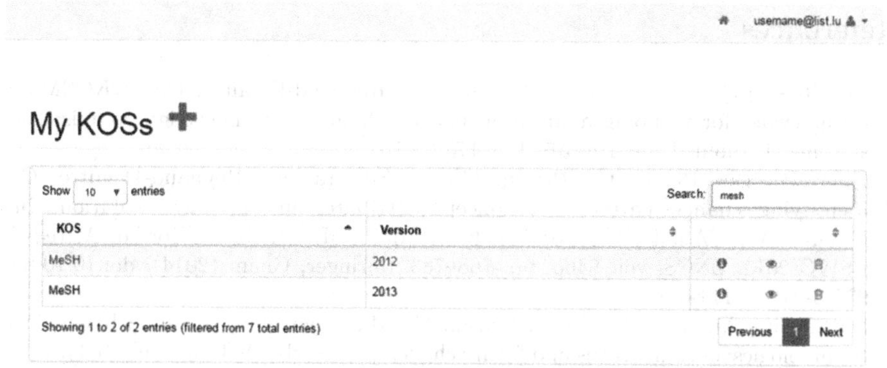

Fig. 2. Store KOS interface

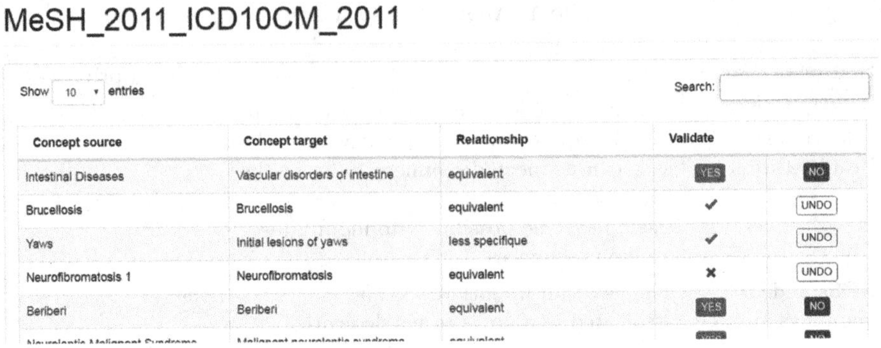

MeSH_2011_ICD10CM_2011

Fig. 3. Validate mappings interface

some errors. In this context, as previously mentioned, DyKOSMap involves human experts to correct possible errors, i.e., each adapted mapping got from our application requires the validation from a domain expert. In this context, we implemented a web interface, depicted in Fig. 3. It is only accessible to expert users. This interface allows to visualize any stored set of mappings established between two KOSs and validate each mapping by "yes" or "no" according to whether the mapping is correct or not. A search box is provided to make the validation of a specific mapping between two concepts easier.

3   Conclusion

This paper described a Web application with advanced user web interface that enables non ICT-experts to use DyKOSMap. We are now working to improve the visualization of KOS and associated data as graphs and to transform the implemented web interface into a restful API to make integration easier.

References

1. Dos Reis, J.C., Pruski, C., Da Silveira, M., Reynaud-Delaître, C.: DyKOSMap: a framework for mapping adaptation between biomedical knowledge organization systems. J. Biomed. Inform. **55**, 153–173 (2015)
2. Dinh, D., Dos Reis, J.C., Pruski, C., Da Silveira, M., Reynaud-Delaître, C.: Identifying change patterns of concept attributes in ontology evolution. In: Presutti, V., d'Amato, C., Gandon, F., d'Aquin, M., Staab, S., Tordai, A. (eds.) ESWC 2014. LNCS, vol. 8465, pp. 768–783. Springer, Cham (2014). doi:10.1007/978-3-319-07443-6_51
3. Da Silveira, M., Dos Reis, J.C., Pruski, C.: Management of dynamic biomedical terminologies: current status and future challenges. Yearb. Med. Inform. **10**(1), 125–133 (2015)

Layout-Aware Semi-automatic Information Extraction for Pharmaceutical Documents

Simon Harmata, Katharina Hofer-Schmitz, Phuong-Ha Nguyen,
Christoph Quix[✉], and Bujar Bakiu

Fraunhofer Institute for Applied Information Technology FIT Schloss Birlinghoven,
53754 Sankt Augustin, Germany
christoph.quix@fit.fraunhofer.de

Abstract. Pharmaceutical companies and regulatory authorities are also affected by the current digitalization process and transform their paper-based, document-oriented communication to a structured, digital information exchange. The documents exchanged so far contain a huge amount of information that needs to be transformed into a structured format to enable a more efficient communication in the future. In such a setting, it is important that the information extracted from documents is very accurate as the information is used in a legal, regulatory process and also for the identification of unknown adverse effects of medicinal products that might be a threat to patients' health. In this paper, we present our layout-aware semi-automatic information extraction system LASIE that combines techniques from rule-based information extraction, flexible data management, and semantic information management in a user-centered design. We applied the system in a case study with an industrial partner and achieved very satisfying results.

1 Introduction

A significant amount of information in the domain of life science and health-care is present only in unstructured documents. Discharge letters from hospitals contain important information about the disease and further treatment of a patient. Although many solutions and standards have been proposed for health data exchange, the discharge letter is still the main medium for communication between hospitals and practitioners in Germany. In the pharmaceutical industry, important information about products is described in *company core data sheets* (CCDS) or *summaries of product characteristics* (SmPC) [17]. These documents contain information about the usage of medicinal products, their risks and adverse effects, their ingredients, etc. The documents have to be maintained by the pharmaceutical company responsible for the manufacturing of the product and have to be provided to the various national authorities for licensing the product. They are also the basis for the package inserts that are provided to the users of the pharmaceutical product. Thus, the same documents have to be maintained in different languages.

Another example for documents in this domain are manufacturing licenses, i.e., documents issued by an authority that authorize a company to produce

M. Da Silveira et al. (Eds.): DILS 2017, LNBI 10649, pp. 71–85, 2017.
https://doi.org/10.1007/978-3-319-69751-2_8

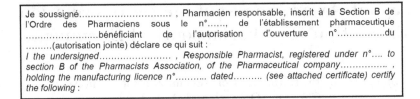

Fig. 1. Example of a multi-lingual document template

medicinal products. These licenses include information about the authorized companies, the issuing date, the license number, the responsible persons, etc. As the licenses are also issued by national authorities, they have different structures and layouts, and are also formulated in various languages. Some of them are a particular challenge because they contain English and another language within the same page, sometimes even within the same paragraph. Figure 1 shows a template of such a document that contains English and French text[1].

Pharmaceutical companies face now the challenge that they have to provide structured information about their products because of the upcoming ISO IDMP standard (Identification of Medicinal Products), which is currently being implemented also by the European Medicines Agency (EMA)[2]. The IDMP standard is basically a huge data model in which information about medicinal products can be represented in a structured form.

Although we referred to the CCDS and SmPC documents above as *unstructured* documents (as they are available in a format of a word processor, e.g., MS Word), they are rather semi-structured documents that follow some guidelines. Most of them (at least within a company) have a similar outline and use similar structures to represent certain information (e.g., tables or bullet point lists). Thus, one approach to get the structured information from the semi-structured documents is to use information extraction (IE). However, the IE approach has to address several challenges:

- The content of the documents is multi-lingual, text fragments with different languages cannot be clearly separated.
- Relevant information is contained in text fragments with a specific layout, e.g., tables for adverse effects.
- Some documents, especially the manufacturing licenses, are only available as scanned paper documents; thus, OCR[3] errors are likely to appear.

---

[1] The example has been taken from http://agence-tst.ansm.sante.fr/html/pdf/3/expor.pdf which is actually an export license of the French authority (ANSM). The manufacturing licenses which we considered in our use case had a similar structure; due to reasons of confidentiality, we cannot show the documents which we processed.

[2] http://www.ema.europa.eu/ema/index.jsp?curl=pages/regulation/general/general_content_000645.jsp.

[3] Optical character recognition.

- Although the documents follow common guidelines or outlines, their structure might be still irregular to some degree. Furthermore, the system should be extensible also for other document types, containing new information items to be extracted.
- The extracted information needs to be consistent with all the present documents that have been submitted to the authorities.
- The information provided to EMA needs to have a very high accuracy as incorrect or incomplete information might have legal consequences.

Various approaches for information extraction from package inserts or similar documents have already been proposed [5,8,11,15,19,20], but they usually rely on Natural Language Processing (NLP) techniques as their focus is on extracting information from natural language text. However, these approaches ignore the fact that the documents have a high regular structure and follow a certain layout to present information. Therefore, a layout-aware information extraction-approach seems to be more promising in this context.

In addition, the terms used in these documents are often terms defined in a controlled vocabulary. For example, MedDRA® is a dictionary that is used by authorities in the pharmaceutical industry for adverse effects. It contains international medical terminology developed under the auspices of the International Conference on Harmonisation of Technical Requirements for Registration of Pharmaceuticals for Human Use (ICH)[4]. Terms extracted from the documents should be matched with the vocabulary terms.

Finally, the approach needs to have an integrated data quality management component, as a high accuracy of the extracted information is required. The prototype system which we developed for a pharmaceutical company, includes an interactive graphical user interface in which the extracted information can be easily verified.

In this paper, we present the overall architecture of our system LASIE (Layout-Aware Semi-automatic Information Extraction) that provides semi-automatic support, focus on the flexible and extensible rule-based extraction system, and discuss the design rationale in developing our prototype. It can process the above mentioned documents (CCDS, Manufacturing Licenses), but it is not limited to these document types as the information extraction can be easily adapted by modifying the extraction rules. Due to confidentiality reasons, we cannot present the details about the datasets used during system development, but we have reconstructed some documents to present the main ideas of our approach.

The paper is structured as follows: the next section gives an overview of our approach, the system architecture, and some details on the datasets. Section 3 explains the main components of the LASIE. The user interface for the integrated data quality management is presented in Sect. 4. Related work is discussed in Sects. 5 and 6 concludes the paper.

---

[4] MedDRA® trademark is owned by IFPMA on behalf of ICH. There are other medical terminology systems (or ontologies) available, but we have to use MedDRA® as it is the terminology required by the authorities.

2   System Overview

The requirements stated in the introduction imply that the system needs to be extensible and flexible to handle various types of documents and to be able to extract several information items from a document. Therefore, the features flexibility and extensibility are immanent features of all components of our system architecture, which is shown in Fig. 2.

Initially, the input documents are parsed and an intermediate HTML-like data model for the documents is created. This representation of documents abstracts from various specific document formats, but still maintains the layout elements which are important for information extraction. Then, LASIE uses a rule-based approach for information extraction [18], implemented by an extensible rule engine.

The workflow of the system according to Fig. 2 can be described as follows: The Data Management Service (DMS) lies at the heart of our system. All modules exchange information with the DMS, which relays the information as structured data objects into the database storage. The principal workflow can be described by three steps: first parse the uploaded input documents for their structure, extract domain-specific information with our rule engine and finally present the results in the web-based user interface for interactive verification of the results.

The next section will describe the components in more detail, but we will first describe the documents that we processed in the case study with our industrial partner.

2.1   Documents in Our Case Study

We verify our system using two sets of documents, provided by our industry partner. The first document type contains detailed medical leaflets from which adverse effects shall be extracted, which were mostly noted using MedDRA®.

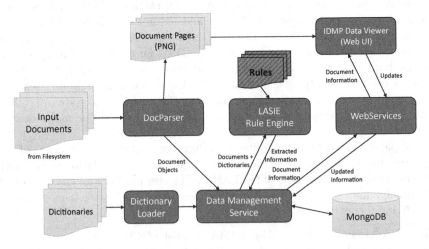

Fig. 2. Overview of the system architecture

MedDRA® is hierarchically organized into five levels: The lowest level describes very specific medical terms as observed in practical use, while each higher level groups several lower level terms into a more general description. An example of the MedDRA® hierarchy can be seen on their website[5]. The highest level contains the system organ classes, which group disorders into different 'functional' areas of the human body, e.g., eye disorders, nervous system disorders.

Company Core Data Sheets (CCDS). The CCDS files are either stored in *doc*- or *docx*-file format and contain information about the contained substances, usage information as well as tables containing adverse effects among others. Our goal is to find all adverse effects and enrich the terms with further information like their MedDRA® ID, the system organ class they belong to as well as the frequency of their occurrence.

We tested our system on 200 CCDS documents of English language (Fig. 3).

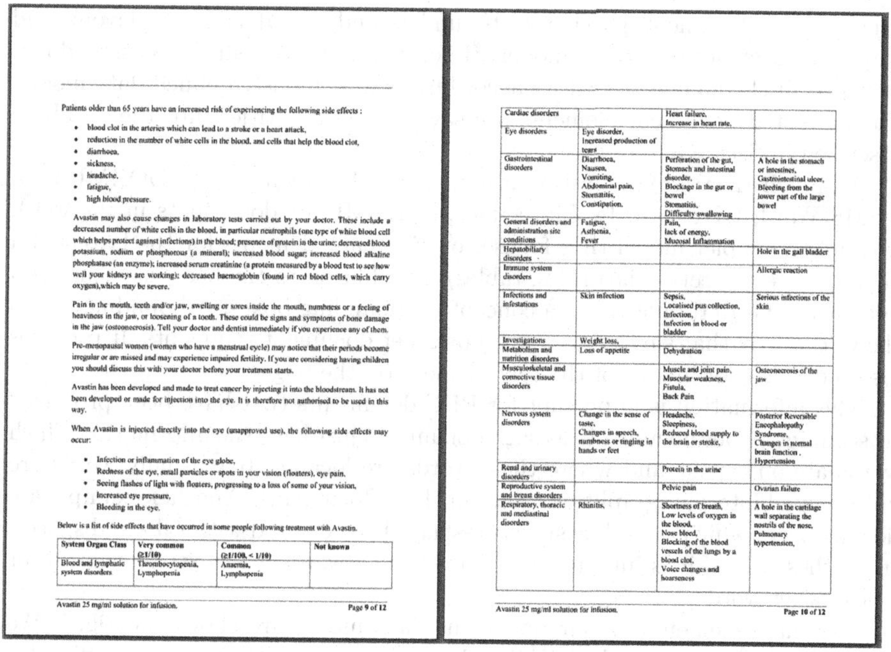
Patients older than 65 years have an increased risk of experiencing the following side effects :

- blood clot in the arteries which can lead to a stroke or a heart attack,
- reduction in the number of white cells in the blood, and cells that help the blood clot,
- diarrhoea,
- sickness,
- headache,
- fatigue,
- high blood pressure.

Avastin may also cause changes in laboratory tests carried out by your doctor. These include a decreased number of white cells in the blood, in particular neutrophils (one type of white blood cell which helps protect against infections) in the blood; presence of protein in the urine; decreased blood potassium, sodium or phosphorous (a mineral); increased blood sugar; increased blood alkaline phosphatase (an enzyme); increased serum creatinine (a protein measured by a blood test to see how well your kidneys are working); decreased haemoglobin (found in red blood cells, which carry oxygen),which may be severe.

Pain in the mouth, teeth and/or jaw, swelling or sores inside the mouth, numbness or a feeling of heaviness in the jaw, or loosening of a tooth. These could be signs and symptoms of bone damage in the jaw (osteonecrosis). Tell your doctor and dentist immediately if you experience any of them.

Pre-menopausal women (women who have a menstrual cycle) may notice that their periods become irregular or are missed and may experience impaired fertility. If you are considering having children you should discuss this with your doctor before your treatment starts.

Avastin has been developed and made to treat cancer by injecting it into the bloodstream. It has not been developed or made for injection into the eye. It is therefore not authorised to be used in this way.

When Avastin is injected directly into the eye (unapproved use), the following side effects may occur:

- Infection or inflammation of the eye globe,
- Redness of the eye, small particles or spots in your vision (floaters), eye pain,
- Seeing flashes of light with floaters, progressing to a loss of some of your vision,
- Increased eye pressure,
- Bleeding in the eye.

Below is a list of side effects that have occurred in some people following treatment with Avastin.

System Organ Class	Very common (≥1/10)	Common (≥1/100, < 1/10)	Not known
Blood and lymphatic system disorders	Thrombocytopenia, Lymphopenia	Anaemia, Lymphopenia	

Avastin 25 mg/ml solution for infusion. Page 9 of 12

Cardiac disorders		Heart failure, Increase in heart rate,	
Eye disorders	Eye disorder, Increased production of tears		
Gastrointestinal disorders	Diarrhoea, Nausea, Vomiting, Abdominal pain, Stomatitis, Constipation.	Perforation of the gut, Stomach and intestinal disorder, Blockage in the gut or bowel Stomatitis, Difficulty swallowing	A hole in the stomach or intestines, Gastrointestinal ulcer, Bleeding from the lower part of the large bowel
General disorders and administration site conditions	Fatigue, Asthenia, Fever	Pain, lack of energy, Mucosal Inflammation	
Hepatobiliary disorders			Hole in the gall bladder
Immune system disorders			Allergic reaction
Infections and infestations	Skin infection	Sepsis, Localised pus collection, Infection, Infection in blood or bladder	Serious infections of the skin
Investigations	Weight loss,		
Metabolism and nutrition disorders	Loss of appetite	Dehydration	
Musculoskeletal and connective tissue disorders		Muscle and joint pain, Muscular weakness, Fistula, Back Pain	Osteonecrosis of the jaw
Nervous system disorders	Change in the sense of taste, Changes in speech, numbness or tingling in hands or feet	Headache, Sleepiness, Reduced blood supply to the brain or stroke,	Posterior Reversible Encephalopathy Syndrome, Changes in normal brain function , Hypertension
Renal and urinary disorders		Protein in the urine	
Reproductive system and breast disorders		Pelvic pain	Ovarian failure
Respiratory, thoracic and mediastinal disorders	Rhinitis,	Shortness of breath, Low levels of oxygen in the blood, Nose bleed, Blocking of the blood vessels of the lungs by a blood clot, Voice changes and hoarseness	A hole in the cartilage wall separating the nostrils of the nose, Pulmonary hypertension,

Avastin 25 mg/ml solution for infusion. Page 10 of 12

Fig. 3. Pages from one of our reconstructed CCDS documents showing the beginning of a typical adverse effects table.

[5] https://www.meddra.org/how-to-use/basics/hierarchy.

Manufacturing Licenses (ML). Although ML documents from different countries share similar information, including the license holder, place of issue and concerned product, the way the information is presented varies a lot. Some documents use tables to show the information, while others use regular text (such as the French document template shown in Fig. 1).

In addition, our dataset contained MLs issued in different European languages, sometimes two in one document as mentioned in the introduction. The documents were often bad quality scans including a few image elements like logos, seals and handwritten signings that might obscure printed text. This results in subpar OCR processing. Contained tables were of implicit nature, i.e., they could not be directly recognized from the scanned PDF files.

Overall, we used 60 ML documents of almost ten different languages.

3   Main Components of LASIE

3.1   Document Parsing

The goal of document parsing is to understand the documents layout and map it to a structured data model. Here, we map our semi-structured documents to single document entities according to a previously defined data model. The extracted document elements are saved as data entities into the database described in Sect. 3.3.

Although there are several data models for documents (e.g., OOXML used by MS Word, ODF used by LibreOffice, or HTML for documents in the web), we apply a simpler model that focuses on the main elements for the layout of a document (e.g., section headings, tables). In addition to the basic elements of a document, our data model has a concept for bounding boxes. A bounding box is the virtual box that surrounds a word or other document fragments. It provides also the X-Y-coordinates of the text element on the page.

This information is important for PDF documents that have been produced by scanning paper documents as such documents just have the information which words are on a page and where these words are located, but usually words are not grouped into paragraphs or tables in these documents. Another example are documents in which table-like structures have been created with tabs and spaces. In all these cases, it is important to know which words are next to, right of, or below other words.

The main elements of our document data model are shown in Fig. 4. We formalized the data model as XML schema, but we just use it as guideline for the JSON representation

On a technical note, to parse MS Word documents (both *doc*- and *docx*-files), we use Apache POI[6], while we use Apache PDFBox[7] for *pdf*-files.

---

[6] https://poi.apache.org/.
[7] https://pdfbox.apache.org/.

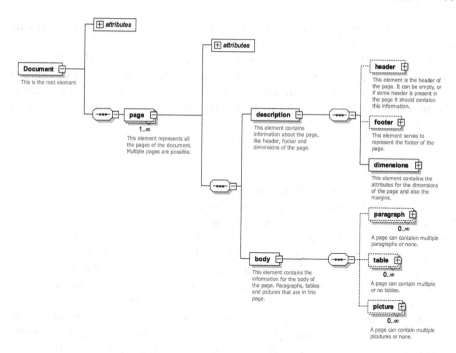

Fig. 4. Main document elements of used XML schema [2]

Company Core Data Sheets. Since MS Word documents follow a very similar structure as our XML schema, document object extraction is very straightforward. Most objects can be directly derived from the document formats. *Doc/docx*-documents are rendered on-view, i.e., the files do not contain any relationships between text elements and pages[8]. Furthermore, things like the section headers' numbering can be derived directly from the file. A section's numbering can be determined through a simple counting loop, though. Since our data model requires the number of pages to match found terms to the contained page, we create *pdf*-versions of our *doc/docx*-files. We also use them to determine the exact word positions and bounding boxes on the pages for presentation of the results.

Manufacturing Licenses. All MLs were scanned and OCR-processed documents of varying quality, including printed and handwritten text, stamps and logos. The OCR processing was done automatically with commercial software ahead of feeding it into our system. As already mentioned, some of them contained two languages alternating with each other, which the software did not always recognize correctly. As the aim of this project was to extract information as is, we did not work on improving the OCR quality. From other projects we

---

[8] The final layout of such documents depend on many factors, including especially the settings of the selected printer. Thus, the layout of a certain page is not stored in the file, but only created when the document is rendered on a screen or printer.

know, that the current commercial tools provide a good quality which is difficult to improve in general.

Opposite to Word files, we start with extraction of words and their bounding boxes. In the next step, words are concatenated into single lines and assigned to pages. Due to complex and variable layout of our *pdf*-files, the recognition of tables and table-like structures is handled by the rule engine described in Sect. 3.2.

3.2 Rule Engine

The rule engine of LASIE is based on the physical structure properties of the documents, where the layout properties are used for extracting information items. One key part in order to keep a modular and flexible system is to separate the rules from the rest of the rule-based framework. The rules for extraction are expressed in a form of declarative programming, i.e., the task and the output of the process is defined. We use DROOLS[9] as rule engine. DROOLS provides a good object-oriented interface in Java (which we used as main programming language in our system) with easy access to elements and properties of rules and facts in the rule engine. One very important feature is the ability to load rules during run-time; thus, changing the extraction rules does not require a recompilation of the software. This was an important requirement of our industrial partner.

The task of the rule engine is to collect the items that make up an information object that should be extracted from the document. In case of adverse effects, it is the name of the adverse effect (a string), a reference to the MedDRA dictionary (if possible), the system organ class, and the frequency of the adverse effect. To achieve this goal, the rule engine needs to match terms of the document with terms from the dictionaries. We distinguish to different cases:

- Mapping from text to semantics: In this case a set of words which need to be mapped is given, e.g. the term *vomiting, diarrhea, headache*.
- Identify terms from dictionary in a paragraph: There the goal is to find the longest possible concatenation of tokens from the paragraph where there are still results in the dictionary.

In the first case, the words are separated by commas and mapped to terms in the dictionary. If the word is not found in the dictionary, a string similarity search is used to propose the user some suggestions. An overview of different approaches for string similarity is given in [10]. There two categories of algorithm, character-based and token-based are distinguished. We used one algorithm for each group, the Jaro-Winkler Algorithm for the first and the Jaccard similarity algorithm for the second one, as these algorithms performed best for our cases. Afterwards, a similarity index for both algorithms is calculated. If this value is above a certain threshold, we assume a possible match.

---

[9] https://www.drools.org/.

String similarity approaches are also applied in the second case, where the longest possible concatenations which matches the dictionary have to be found. There, in case of a high string similarity, the terms are added to the final result.

The rules for the rule engine are defined in separate files, which can be grouped in preprocessing, extraction and output. For the definition of the rules, it is important that the order of applying the rules do not affect the result, due to pattern matching principles which are usually used by rule engines. Moreover, the rules have to respect the hierarchy of elements in the document, i.e., constructive rules which do not break the current hierarchy but only improve or enrich it, have been generated.

The basic process of the rule engine is as follows:

1. Prepare a session: The rule engine finds all rule files for a given session name (e.g., the type of documents to be processed).
2. Load the rule files.
3. Compile the rules; this is performed by the DROOLS framework.
4. Initialize the working memory of the session with the data, i.e., the document structure created by the document parser is inserted as factsto the rule engine.
5. Fire the rules. This process is based on the conditions of each rule. Rules can be fired multiple times, and the process will continue until no rule can be fired anymore.
6. In the last step, the result from the working memory is obtained (i.e., the derived facts or extracted information) and transformed into a data object for the data management service. Here, it is important to note that the structure of the resulting data object cannot be defined in general beforehand. This depends on the type of information to be extracted. As the rules can be modified by the users of the system, they can also change the structure of the resulting data object. Thus, the schema of the data object needs to be flexible, which we will discuss in the next subsection.

Listing 1 shows an example of a rule that extracts the authorization number from a manufacturing license. These are usually scanned documents with a table structure. In another rule, the document type has already been recognized; therefore, we first retrieve a document of type 'MLDocument'. Then, we retrieve a line with its bounding box (bb) and check whether it contains a string that indicates an authorization number. In the next step, we retrieve a line (l2) which is on the same page and has a bounding box (bb2) which approximately right of the previous bounding box bb. In the conclusion part of the rule, we store the extracted information in our result data structure, including a score.

For interpreting the results of the rules, a candidate score approach is used. That means each extracted information by the rules is considered as candidate answer which gets a value between 0 and 100 based on the properties or conditions. The final result is then a collection of several candidate items with corresponding scores, which can be used in the User Interface to present the results.

Listing 1. Extract authorization number

```
rule "Authorisation Number"
when
  m: MLDocument($d : document)
  l: Line( bb : boundingBox ) from $d.getLine()
  eval(l.hasSubstring("Authorisation number") || l.hasSubstring("Number
      of license") || l.hasSubstring("Number of permit") ||
      l.hasSubstring("Authorization number"))
  l2 : Line( boundingBox.page == bb.page, bb2 : boundingBox ) from
      $d.getLine()
  eval(bb2.fuzzyIsRightOf(bb))
then
  List listLine = getAllLinesInSector(1, $d, 1, bb.getHeight(),
      bb.getWidth());
  CandidateNumber n = new CandidateNumber();
  n.setType("CandidateNumber");
  n.setLines(listLine);
  n.setScore(100);
  n.setRelationship("Document_ref", m.getDocumentRef());
  m.regNumber.add(n);
end
```

3.3 Data Management Service

Our system consists of separate independent modules that exchange data via the central data management service (DMS). As stated above, the system should be extensible and adaptable for other use cases and not limited to the specific document types considered initially in the project.

Therefore, the aim was to provide an easy to use, extensible common data structure, that should be able to represent different types of data objects. For example, the data structure needs to be able to represent the document structure as described above by the XML schema as well as the result objects of information extraction. In case of CCDS documents, this is a list of adverse effects with links to their corresponding representation in the MedDRA dictionary.

One possible approach could have been to define an XML schema (or JSON data structure) for each of the relevant data objects. However, as discussed above, this is not possible as the rules for information extraction can be changed by the user and the structure of the extracted can vary between different rule sets. Therefore, we decided to design a generic structure of data objects which can represent any kind of data model.

The core of our DMS is the generic DataEntity which is a class with the following members:

ID: the ID of the object,
type: a string denoting the type of the object,
version: a version number,
relationships: a map that relates a relationship name with a list of related objects, and
properties: a map that relates a property name with a list of values.

The DMS provides storage and retrieval mechanisms for data objects. Each module only uses the interface of the DMS for data access. In our prototype system, we decided to use MongoDB as the underlying storage system, but the generic data structure could be also mapped to other data management systems.

The data objects in our model are immutable, that means that each change to an object will create a new version of an object. Thus, the database might contain objects with the same ID but with different versions. One reason for this is to enable traceability of all changes that have been applied to data objects. This is especially important for the interaction in the user interface; it should be possible to trace the changes and to see who is responsible for which change.

To access the data, the DMS provides several query functions, e.g., retrieving an object with a specific ID, retrieving all objects of a certain type, or retrieving objects with certain properties or relationships. These query functions are wrapped as REST services such that the web-based user interface can easily access the data that has been generated by the document parser and the rule engine.

4   Web-Based User Interface

We display the extracted information using an interactive web-based user interface (UI). A key feature of the web application is the ability to show the source documents and the extracted information next to each other, thereby enabling the easy verification of the extracted information (as illustrated in Fig. 5). Requirement discussions with our industry partner revealed the need to review and modify the results by experts due to high accuracy demand before accepting the results. Our system enables the user to be in control of the information extraction, while the process is transparent, reliable and repeatable.

On the left-hand side of the UI, the original document is displayed, with adverse effects found framed in different colors indicating their annotation status. The annotations are shown on the right side and can be changed by the user. Both parts of the UI are linked, i.e., when the user clicks on a frame on the left side, the corresponding extracted information item will be shown on the right and vice versa. This enables easy verification of the extracted information. Once a document has been checked by two experts and marked as 'accepted', its terms are permanently accepted into the database.

5   Related Work

Very similar work to our overall approach of layout-aware information extraction has been presented in [1]. The described system automatically determines posology, side effects and indications from Portuguese medical leaflets by NLP methods. The design is based on six steps: text preprocessing, a document reader, a general natural language processing module, a named entity recognition, relation extraction and an information consumer step.

However, for a well working automatic classification tool usually a huge amount of pre-labeled training data is necessary. In case of low quality data,

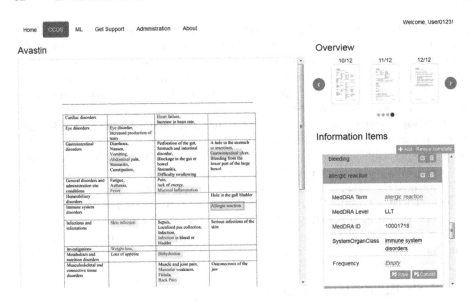

Fig. 5. Example showing the UI during quality check, with fully annotated terms colored in green and incomplete in orange. The example shows the term 'allergic reactions' for which no 'frequency of occurrence' could be found. The table header with this information was on the previous page.

the accuracy of these systems usually decreases drastically. Since in our application, the accuracy and understandability of the extraction rules are some of the key points of the system, we focused on a rule-based system with user interaction to enable a very high accuracy independent of the quality or availability of training data.

In the following, we will briefly discuss related work to the different components of our system.

Information Extraction. Information Extraction (IE) has been extensively studied since the late 1980s [18]. It describes the process of automatically retrieving structured information from machine-readable, semi- or unstructured documents. Structures include types like *(named) entities*, *relationships* between two entities, *layout entities* of documents and *ontologies*.

Typically, the extraction of information is done in two steps: first extract domain-unspecific structure from the documents and then use the results to extract domain-specific elements. We also follow this general pattern and divide the process in document parsing and rule-based extraction.

Document Parsing. Document parsing is domain-independent and once implemented it can be applied to new sources with similar layout without major changes. Partially structured documents, like newspaper articles, journal papers, technical documentation and medical leaflets, often follow an already defined rough format style. With file formats like *doc/docx* and *html* it is relatively easy to extract structures like *sections, section headers, paragraphs* or *tables*, as the file format already incorporates tags describing those. More refined methods are needed to classify such structures from PDF documents and simple text files.

Hierarchical document parsing via top-down approaches, often using image processing methods, have been first proposed by [6, 16] and more recent by [7]. Table understanding has been studied independently as part of general document recognition. A comparison of various techniques can be found in [9].

Rule-Based Information Extraction. Opposite to statistical methods for information extraction, rule-based methods are easy to formulate and understand by a human reader.

There are two possibilities to obtain rules: The first one is to use rule-based systems or to use learning systems. At the very beginning rule-based systems were used. Nowadays more and more learning systems appear. Statistical methods to transform the task into a classification task use for example the Hidden Markov Model, Conditional Markov Model or Random Fields, see [14]. However, for well-working learning systems usually enough training data has to be available. Moreover, even though for rule-based approaches it might be hard to define every case, they can easily be implemented. A further advantage is, that the process and not the way to achieve the goal is coded, which enables an easier expression of the solution. Furthermore, rule-based systems are fast and can be easily optimized. Examples for systems based on rules are GATE [4], TextMarker [13] and SystemT [3].

Data Management. For an efficient data management, it is especially important to use a suitable data model to efficiently support queries. The most crucial point there is to use a generic data model as we cannot fix the schema of the extracted data beforehand. In [12], a generic data model is presented. There, a generic model management which serves as an abstraction of particular meta-models and preserves as much of the original features of modeling constructs as possible is developed. As the goal there is to support model management operations, the generic data model focuses on a detailed representation of features of different modeling languages. Here, we aim at providing a flexible and extensible representation of data objects and do not deal with the details of modeling languages.

6   Conclusion and Discussion of Results

In this paper, we presented a complete system to extract specified information from medical documents, using efficient methods for extraction, data storage & retrieval and reviewing. We applied the system to real use case of our industrial partner.

The results from this use case and the feedback from our industrial partner were very promising. In contrast to a complete manual extraction process, the proposed system provides a repeatable and traceable extraction procedure. Especially, the web-based UI with an integrated visualization of source document and extracted information was considered as an important component of the system. Such a link between extracted information and source data cannot be easily established in a manual approach.

We have shown that information extraction from documents is possible with adaptable methods. Data quality in our approach is high as the extracted data can be matched with controlled vocabularies.

The rule-based extraction process was also able to reveal inconsistencies in the source documents. For example, some documents contained inconsistent information (value X for a certain property was stated on one page, whereas another value Y was stated for the same property on another page). Other examples of revealed problems in the source data was the use of an outdated terminology in the documents, as controlled vocabularies also evolve.

With the data management service and the generic data model, we developed a flexible framework for data processing. This service is also a core component of other projects in our group, as it provides an easy to use yet efficient way to manage data. Furthermore we intend to extend the data management framework by an common and flexible query mechanism and by an meta data enrichment.

An interesting feature for future work is to use the user input to learn rules for the extraction process. If a user edits the extracted information always in the same way, this might be expressed in a rule.

Acknowledgements. This work has been partially funded by the German Federal Ministry of Education and Research (BMBF) (project HUMIT, http://humit.de/, grant no. 01IS14007A).

References

1. Aguiar, B.L., Mendes, E., Ferreira, L. Information extraction from medication leaflets. Ph.D. thesis, Master thesis, FEUP, Porto (2012)
2. Bakiu, B.: Layout-aware semantic information extraction from semi-structured documents. RWTH Aachen University, Master (2015)
3. Chiticariu, L., Krishnamurthy, R., Li, Y., Raghavan, S., Reiss, F.R., Vaithyanathan, S.: SystemT: an algebraic approach to declarative information extraction. In: Proceeding 48th Annual Meeting Assocation Computational Linguistics, ACL 2010, pp. 128–137. Association for Computational Linguistics, Stroudsburg, PA, USA (2010)
4. Cunningham, H., Maynard, D., Bontcheva, K., Tablan, V., Aswani, N., Roberts, I., Gorrell, G., Funk, A., Roberts, A., Damljanovic, D., et al.: Developing language processing components with GATE version 7 (a user guide). University of Sheffield, UK (2013). https://gate.ac.uk/sale/tao/index.html
5. Duke, J.D., Friedlin, J.: ADESSA: a real-time decision support service for delivery of semantically coded adverse drug event data. In: AMIA Annual Symposium Proceedings, vol. 2010, 177–181 (2010)

6. Ejiri, M.: Knowledge-based approaches to practical image processing. In: Industrial Applications of Machine Intelligence and Vision (MIV-89), Tokyo, 10–12 April 1989, p. 1 (1989)

7. Gao, L., Tang, Z., Lin, X., Liu, Y., Qiu, R., Wang, Y.: Structure extraction from PDF-based book documents. In: Proceedings of the 11th Annual International ACM/IEEE Joint Conference on Digital libraries, pp. 11–20. ACM (2011)

8. Ge, C., Zhang, Y., Duan, H., Li, H.: Identification of adverse drug events in chinese clinical narrative text. In: Park, J.J.J.H., Pan, Y., Chao, H.-C., Yi, G. (eds.) Ubiquitous Computing Application and Wireless Sensor. LNEE, vol. 331, pp. 605–612. Springer, Dordrecht (2015). doi:10.1007/978-94-017-9618-7_62

9. Gobel, M., Hassan, T., Oro, E., Orsi, G.: ICDAR 2013 Table Competition. In: 2013 12th International Conference on Document Analysis and Recognition, pp. 1449–1453. IEEE, August 2013

10. Gomaa, W.H., Fahmy, A.A.: A survey of text similarity approaches. Int. J. Comput. Appl. **68**(13), 13–18 (2013)

11. Iqbal, E., Mallah, R., Jackson, R.G., Ball, M., Ibrahim, Z.M., Broadbent, M., Dzahini, O., Stewart, R., Johnston, C., Dobson, R.J.B.: Identification of adverse drug events from free text electronic patient records and information in a large mental health case register. PLoS One **10**(8), e0134208 (2015)

12. Kensche, D., Quix, C., Chatti, M.A., Jarke, M.: *GeRoMe*: a generic role based metamodel for model management. In: Spaccapietra, S., et al. (eds.) Journal on Data Semantics VIII. LNCS, vol. 4380, pp. 82–117. Springer, Heidelberg (2007). doi:10.1007/978-3-540-70664-9_4

13. Kluegl, P., Atzmueller, M., Puppe, F.: TextMarker: a tool for rule-based information extraction. In: Chiarcos, C., de Castilho, R.E., Stede, M. (eds.) Proceedings of the Biennial GSCL Conference 2009, 2nd UIMA@GSCL Workshop, pp. 233–240. Gunter Narr Verlag (2009). http://ki.informatik.uni-wuerzburg.de/papers/pkluegl/2009-GSCL-TextMarker.pdf

14. Lafferty, J.D., McCallum, A., Pereira, F.C.N., Fields, C.R.: Probabilistic models for segmenting and labeling sequence data. In: Proceedings of the Eighteenth International Conference on Machine Learning, ICML 2001, pp. 282–289. Morgan Kaufmann Publishers Inc., San Francisco, CA, USA (2001)

15. Meystre, S., Haug, P.J.: Natural language processing to extract medical problems from electronic clinical documents: performance evaluation. J. Biomed. Inform. **39**(6), 589–599 (2006)

16. Nagy, G., Seth, S.: Hierarchical representation of optically scanned documents. In: International Conference on Pattern Recognition, vol. 1, pp. 347–349 (1984)

17. Nahler, G.: Dictionary of Pharmaceutical Medicine. Springer, Vienna (2009). doi:10.1007/978-3-211-89836-9

18. Sarawagi, S.: Information extraction. Found. Trends® Databases **1**(3), 261–377 (2007)

19. Thompson, C.A., Califf, M.E., Mooney, R.J.: Active learning for natural language parsing and information extraction. In: ICML, pp. 406–414 (1999)

20. Wang, X., Chase, H., Markatou, M., Hripcsak, G., Friedman, C.: Selecting information in electronic health records for knowledge acquisition. J. Biomed. Inform. **43**(4), 595–601 (2010)

Enabling Data Integration Using MIPMap

Giorgos Stoilos, Despoina Trivela, Vasilis Vassalos, Tassos Venetis[✉],
and Yannis Xarchakos

Department of Informatics, Athens University of Economics and Business,
Athens, Greece
avenet@aueb.gr

Abstract. In previous work we have analysed the infrastructure of the
Human Brain Project Medical Informatics Platform focusing on the challenges related to dataintegration based on a visual data exchange tool,
called MIPMap. In this paper we present new MIPMap features that
enhance the integration process and data access.

1 Introduction

Brain research has received significant attention during the last decades and is
one of the most important challenges of the 21st century science. The Human
Brain Project (HBP) aims to develop technologies that enhance the scientific
research related to human brain. Towards this effort six ICT platforms are being
developed, dedicated to Neuroinformatics, Brain Simulation, High Performance
Computing, Medical Informatics, Neuromorphic Computing and Neurorobotics.

The goal of the Medical Informatics Platform[1] (MIP) is to gain fundamen-
tal insights into brain function through convergence between ICT and biology.
This will lead to new diagnostics categories, supported by strong hypotheses of
disease causation, which will encourage the development of new treatments for
brain diseases. The MIP research infrastructure will also enable the federation of
neuroscience data from all over the world, the integration of the data in unifying
models and simulations of the brain, validation of the results against empirical
data from biology and medicine, and allow the fruits of this work to be made
available to the global scientific community. In order to meet its goal the MIP
transforms medical records into research data, extracts knowledge and builds
models of brain diseases. The system provides dedicated services to researchers
to carry out neuro-epidemiological and biological investigations on federated
clinical data, without moving them from their storage sites and compromising
patient privacy following national legislation and institutional ethics.

MIP is roughly composed of three different layers. Following a top-down
approach the first one is the Web Portal, which is the user interface of the
platform, providing access to the Platform's analytic functionalities. The second
layer is the Federation Layer that is responsible for federating the queries posed
over the Web Portal to proper queries that are executed over the hospitals'
datasets. Additionally, it is responsible for collecting and merging the relevant

---

[1] http://mip.humanbrainproject.eu.

M. Da Silveira et al. (Eds.): DILS 2017, LNBI 10649, pp. 86–93, 2017.
https://doi.org/10.1007/978-3-319-69751-2_9

queries' answers. The third layer, is the Local Layer which is responsible for exposing to the platform data originating from hospitals and research centers, creating the so called Local Data Store Mirrors (LDSMs). Each hospital's LDSM is populated with brain features [2], extracted from MRI images, integrated with Electronic Health Records (EHR data) under a common schema, after having been properly anonymized and acts as connection point to the Federation Layer.

In our previous work [21] we have presented how the MIP architecture meets Data Integration. Regarding gathering disparate hospital and research data and integrating them under the common MIP schema we have presented a visual data exchange tool called MIPMap.[2] MIPMap has been developed, based on the open source mapping tool ++Spicy [11], in order to better meet the needs of HBP and includes an improved mapping execution engine capable to deal with the complexity and size of HBP data transformations. MIPMap is used on the Local Layer and is responsible for integrating EHR data and brain features to a common MIP schema and thus populating each hospitals LDSM, made available to the platform. This integration process is formalized through Tuple Generating Dependencies (TGDs) [1] that are executed using the chase [1].

In the current paper, we present solutions and implemented techniques that extend MIPMap beyond a data exchange engine and enhance interoperability and accessing the hospital data. Our motivation lies in enabling collaboration in designing the mapping that will perform the integration of data, allowing inter-operability through the use of ontologies and finally defining policies for secure sharing of information. Hence, we describe some new features that strengthen the acquisition and re-usability of clinical and research data within HBP.

2   WebMIPMap

WebMIPMap[3] is a web application built as an extension of the MIPMap desktop application that offers schema mapping utilities. WebMIPMap provides an easy to use web interface where correspondences between schemata can be defined by simply drawing lines between two tree-form representations and generates declarative representations, under the formalism of TGD rules. Its purpose is allowing registered users of the HBP to create mappings between the MIP schema and other (external) schemata and/or ontologies. These mappings can be used to reformulate queries posed using terminology of the external schemata to terms of the MIP schema and hence allow queries posed using external schemata to be posed in the MIP.

Although MIPMap focuses equally on the generation of the rules that define the mappings between a source and a target schema as well as on the exchange of data instances between them, WebMIPMap does not provide data exchange capabilities. The reason for that is that this would imply that hospital data would have to leave the hospital LDSM, and hence the "no move no copy" policy

---

[2] https://github.com/aueb-wim/MIPMap.

[3] https://github.com/aueb-wim/WebMIPMap.

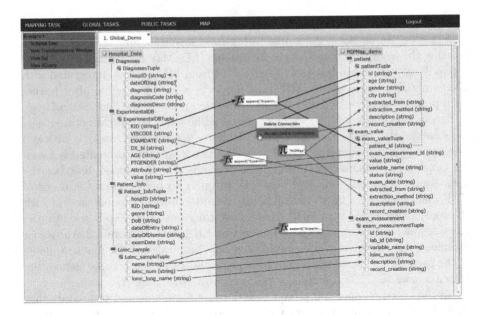

Fig. 1. Mapping task in WebMIPMap (Color figure online)

imposed due to data privacy, would be violated. Note however, that mapping tasks created with WebMIPMap can be downloaded and used by MIPMap.

WebMIPMap (Fig. 1) expresses a mapping between a source and a target schema through graphically defining the correspondences (lines) between them, as well as join conditions, constraints and functional transformations. The tool supports the creation of n:m correspondences allowing complex transformation functions and the assignment of constant values or function generated values. Selection conditions can also be applied on the tables of the source schema to allow only tuples that satisfy certain criteria to be used in the data exchange process.

2.1 Collaborative Data Integration

What is special about WebMIPMap is that it allows collaboration [13,23] among its users allowing them to create, validate and reuse their mapping tasks collaboratively. Users (depending on their role) are able to view, modify and adopt mappings from online stored mapping tasks.

More precisely, an administrator user can create mappings and make them available to all users. Such mappings are called "global" and every user is able to view them and moreover edit them in their own workspace. Additionally, users can store the (possibly) altered global mapping to their own workspace. When a user loads a global mapping all the correspondences are presented using green dotted lines, as can be seen in Fig. 1. In the following the user can either endorse or delete these lines in order to create his own mapping task. As soon as the user saves his work, all connections are represented by the same color and there is no distinction between the user-generated and the global correspondences.

In addition to the administrator's global mappings, WebMIPMap supports the "users I trust" feature. This feature allows users to load, view and edit user-defined mappings of other users (not necessarily administrators) that are called "public". Users can submit trust requests to other WebMIPMap users using a search by name operation. In the following the users accepting the request can either accept or reject the request, just like in social media. If a user accepts an incoming trust request, access is granted to the sender to view his public mapping tasks. Again, public mapping tasks are loaded using different color (blue) and users can endorse or delete each correspondence.

In case multiple (trusted) users have made public on their workspace the same mapping task[4], that however contains different correspondences and hence leads to different TGDs, trusted users can request for a mapping task recommendation. The recommended mapping task is created automatically considering all the currently available correspondences. More precisely, a weight is given to each mapping task's correspondence that ends to each target attribute and the one with the highest weight is selected. The weight is computed as the average of the following normalized metrics and reflects the overall quality of the mapping with respect to the user's contribution and credibility:

1. *page rank* [14], that is a very popular algorithm used to measure users' importance inside a network,
2. *user credibility*, that is a metric of the user's reputation calculated as the division of the number of accepted connections of this user by the total number of connections he has created in his mapping tasks,
3. *connection credibility*, that provides a reputation score of a single correspondence inside a (same) mapping task and is calculated as the division of the number of times a specific correspondence appears[5] by the total number of different correspondences appearing in all the same mapping tasks.
4. *user's total connections*, that is a metric that calculates the total number of connections that a user has created in this mapping task.

Again, as soon as the user reviews and then endorses the aggregated mapping scenario (or part of it), this is saved on his workspace. Finally, in order to enhance collaboration, when a user selects a mapping scenario he is informed about the credibility of other users with similar mappings. The credibility of a user is computed by taking into account the number of connections that have been endorsed by other users.

---

[4] Same mapping tasks are the ones that have the same tables and attributes as source and target schemata respectively.

[5] Two correspondences are the same if they have the same (source and) target attributes and in case they contain functions or constants they are also the same.

3   Mapping to Ontologies

Another new feature of MIPMap is that of ontological support [6]. More precisely, MIPMap can be used to create mapping tasks where the target schema is that of an ontology in OWL 2 [12] while the source schema can be either a collection of csv files (each file corresponds to a table) or a relational schema, as usual. The benefit of this feature is twofold. First of all, MIPMap can be used as data exchange tool that can populate an ontology with instances of relational or csv data. Moreover, MIPMap can be used as a visual mapping tool to create R2RML mappings [5] that can be exported and used by any Ontology-Based Data Access system that supports R2RML, like IQAROS [20] and Ontop [16]. R2RML is a W3C recommended language for expressing customized mappings from relational databases to RDF datasets.

The major challenge we had to overcome was to decide the most appropriate way to represent the ontology elements, namely the Classes, Object and Datatype Properties to relational tables, that are the means of representing relations in MIPMap. Numerous approaches have been presented in the literature [3,4,22] but we have followed the most simple approach; that of converting the three aformentioned elements in the target ontology to database tables. For every Class a table with one column is created that is intended to hold the names of the corresponding individuals of the class, while for every Property a table with two columns is created; the first one holds the subject instances of the property, and the second the objects instances of the property (or a string value in case a Datatype Property is represented in either the subject or the object).

For example, consider the class Patient of the SNOMED[6] ontology. A one-column table is created for the class to be filled with patients identification numbers. Consider now, that a user creates a correspondence from attribute *patient_ipp* of demographics table to the Patient class. This will lead to the creation of the following TGD:

$$\text{demographics}(patient\_ipp, gender, city) \rightarrow \text{Patient}(patient\_ipp) \qquad (1)$$

Having created the above TGD the user can now either perform a data exchange operation where an owl file can be exported containing instances for the Patient class or an R2RML script can be exported that can be used with OBDA tools. The following R2RML script results from TGD (1):

```
@prefix rr: <http://www.w3.org/ns/r2rml#>.
@prefix snomed: <http://www.ihtsdo.org/#>.
⟨#TripleMap1⟩
rr:logicalTable    [rr:tableName "demographics" ];
rr:subjectMap      [rr:template "{patient_ipp}";
                    rr:class snomed:Patient];
```

---

[6] http://www.snomed.org.

4   Modelling Access Restrictions

Many modern applications relying on data exchange, like MIP, require to define policies for secure sharing of information. Research in the area has resulted in several access control models [7, 10] and languages [19] as well as in access control systems for various application domains [8, 9, 15, 18]. In the case of MIP we propose an access control mechanism that embodies the basic concepts of Role-Based Access Control (RBAC) [17], approved as a standard by the American National Standards Insitute (ANSI) [7]. According to this model access to system resources is restricted w.r.t. to user roles that are granted specific permissions. Consequently, different users of MIP may be assigned to different permissions over its resources (data or services).

The purpose of the proposed access control mechanism is to filter the information deriving from different hospitals that will be available to the end-user through MIP services. When a WebMIPMap user maps his dataset to an ontology, he will have the choice to determine his own restrictions concerning the availability of this dataset. For example, he may choose that only trusted users that are administrators can have access to the instances of Patient class. Next, his restrictions are translated into access control rules which are defined by using the ontology vocabulary. Therefore, the definition of the rules uniquely depends on the ontology language and on the requirements of each provider. User roles are described by (new) concepts inserted in the ontology and are described as subclasses of the concept Role. We define the classes TU (trusted user), AU (administrator user), DU (developer user), GU (general user) which can be further subcategorized to Psyciatrists, Neurologists, Geneticists and Pathologists. Finally, the access rules are considered as ontological axioms and are taken into account by the reasoning engine during ontology-based query answering.

Example 1. Consider that userA maps his data to an ontology that includes the roles hasDescription($exid, descr$), examMeasurement($exid, mesid$). Moreover, assume he wishes to allow access to psyciatric measurements only to psyciatrists. This is encoded in the following access rule:

$$\text{Psyciatrist}(user), \text{hasDescription}(eid, \text{``}PsyciatricExam\text{''}), \text{subject}(access, user),$$
$$\text{object}(access, eid) \rightarrow access.\text{hasDescription}(exid, \text{``}PsyciatricExam\text{''})$$

Note that variable *user* identifies the subject issuing the access request and that the object of the request is variable *eid* in hasDescription (eid, "$PsyciatricExam$"). Assume that userA makes his mapping global and his data available to other MIP users. Next, userB executes a query over the dataset of userA, asking for the measurements of any psyciatric exam:

$$\text{hasDescription}(exid, \text{``}PsyciatricExam\text{''}), \text{examMeasurement}(exid, mesid)$$
$$\rightarrow Q(mesid)$$

By taking into account the access rule the following transformations are performed:

$$\text{access.hasDescription}(exid, \text{``}PsyciatricExam\text{''}), \text{examMeasurement}(exid, mesid)$$
$$\rightarrow Q(mesid)$$

$$\text{Psyciatrist}(UserB), \text{hasDescription}(exid, \text{``}PsyciatricExam\text{''}),$$
$$\text{subject}(access, UserB), \text{object}(access, exid), \text{examMeasurement}(exid, mesid)$$
$$\rightarrow Q(mesid)$$

If userB is a registered psyciatrist then the ontology includes an assertion of the form Psyciatrist($UserB$). Otherwise, his query returns an empty answerset. ◇

5   Conclusions

We have presented new features integrated in MIPMap, a novel visual data exchange tool. Overall, the extensions enforce MIP's functionality and services by enabling the creation of schema mappings through a collaborative Web experience, the use of ontologies to describe (medical) data, and finally, the definition of filtering conditions on data access.

Acknowledgment. The research leading to these results has received funding from the European Union's Horizon 2020 research and innovation programme under grant agreement No. 720270 (HBP SGA1).

References

1. Abiteboul, S., Hull, R., Vianu, V.: Foundations of Databases. Addison-Wesley, Massachusetts (1995)
2. Ashburner, J., Friston, K.J.: Diffeomorphic registration using geodesic shooting and Gauss-Newton optimisation. NeuroImage **55**(3), 954–967 (2011)
3. Astrova, I., Kalja, A.: Automatic transformation of sql relational databases to owl ontologies. WEBIST **2**(2008), 131–136 (2008)
4. Dadjoo, M., Kheirkhah, E.: An approach for transforming of relational databases to owl ontology. arXiv preprint arXiv:1502.05844 (2015)
5. Das, S., Sundara, S., Cyganiak, R.: R2RML: RDB to RDF mapping language (2012)
6. Eleftherios, F.: Extending a data integration tool with ontologies. Thesis report in Master of Science in Information Systems, Athens University of Economics and Business, October 2016
7. Ferraiolo, D.F., Sandhu, R., Gavrila, S., Kuhn, D.R., Chandramouli, R.: Proposed NIST standard for role-based access control. ACM Trans. Inf. Syst. Secur. **4**(3), 224–274 (2001)
8. García-Crespo, Á., Gómez-Berbís, J.M., Colomo-Palacios, R., Alor-Hernández, G.: Securontology: a semantic web access control framework. Comput. Stand. Interfaces **33**(1), 42–49 (2011)

9. Jain, A., Farkas, C.: Secure resource description framework: an access control model. In: Proceedings of the Eleventh ACM Symposium on Access Control Models and Technologies, pp. 121–129. ACM (2006)
10. Li, N., Mitchell, J.C.: DATALOG with constraints: a foundation for trust management languages. In: Dahl, V., Wadler, P. (eds.) PADL 2003. LNCS, vol. 2562, pp. 58–73. Springer, Heidelberg (2003). doi:10.1007/3-540-36388-2_6
11. Marnette, B., et al.: ++Spicy: an OpenSource Tool for second-generation schema mapping and data exchange. PVLDB 4(12), 1438–1441 (2011)
12. Motik, B., Grau, B.C., Horrocks, I., Wu, Z., Fokoue, A., Lutz, C.: OWL 2 Web Ontology Language Profiles. W3C Recommendation, 27 October 2009
13. Quoc Viet Nguyen, H., Luong, X.H., Miklós, Z., Quan, T.T., Aberer, K.: Collaborative schema matching reconciliation. In: Meersman, R., Panetto, H., Dillon, T., Eder, J., Bellahsene, Z., Ritter, N., De Leenheer, P., Dou, D. (eds.) OTM 2013. LNCS, vol. 8185, pp. 222–240. Springer, Heidelberg (2013). doi:10.1007/978-3-642-41030-7_14
14. Page, L., Brin, S., Motwani, R., Winograd, T.: The pagerank citation ranking: Bringing order to the web. Technical report, Stanford InfoLab (1999)
15. Reddivari, P., Finin, T., Joshi, A.: Policy-based access control for an RDF store. In: Proceedings of the Policy Management for the Web Workshop, vol. 120, pp. 78–83 (2005)
16. Rodríguez-Muro, M., Kontchakov, R., Zakharyaschev, M.: Ontology-based data access: *Ontop* of databases. In: Alani, H., Kagal, L., Fokoue, A., Groth, P., Biemann, C., Parreira, J.X., Aroyo, L., Noy, N., Welty, C., Janowicz, K. (eds.) ISWC 2013. LNCS, vol. 8218, pp. 558–573. Springer, Heidelberg (2013). doi:10.1007/978-3-642-41335-3_35
17. Sandhu, R.S., Coyne, E.J., Feinstein, H.L., Youman, C.E.: Role-based access control models. IEEE Comput. 29(2), 38–47 (1996)
18. Shields, B., Molloy, O., Lyons, G., Duggan, J.: Using semantic rules to determine access control for web services. In: Proceedings of the 15th International Conference on World Wide Web, WWW 2006, Edinburgh, Scotland, UK, 23–26 May 2006, pp. 913–914 (2006)
19. Tonti, G., Bradshaw, J.M., Jeffers, R., Montanari, R., Suri, N., Uszok, A.: Semantic web languages for policy representation and reasoning: a comparison of KAoS, Rei, and Ponder. In: Fensel, D., Sycara, K., Mylopoulos, J. (eds.) ISWC 2003. LNCS, vol. 2870, pp. 419–437. Springer, Heidelberg (2003). doi:10.1007/978-3-540-39718-2_27
20. Venetis, T., Stoilos, G., Stamou, G.: Query extensions and incremental query rewriting for OWL 2 QL ontologies. J. Data Semant. 3(1), 1–23 (2014)
21. Venetis, T., Vassalos, V.: Data integration in the human brain project. In: Ashish, N., Ambite, J.-L. (eds.) DILS 2015. LNCS, vol. 9162, pp. 28–36. Springer, Cham (2015). doi:10.1007/978-3-319-21843-4_3
22. Vysniauskas, E., Nemuraite, L.: Transforming ontology representation from owl to relational database. Inform. Technol. Control 35(3) (2015)
23. Zhang, C.J., Chen, L., Jagadish, H.V., Cao, C.C.: Reducing uncertainty of schema matching via crowdsourcing. Proc. VLDB Endowment 6(9), 757–768 (2013)

Interactive Map Visualization System Based on Integrated Semi-structured and Structured Healthcare Data

Milena Frtunić Gligorijević[1(✉)], Darko Puflović[1],
Evgenija Stevanoska[2], Tatjana Jevtović Stoimenov[3], Goran Velinov[4],
and Leonid Stoimenov[1]

[1] Faculty of Electronic Engineering, University of Niš, Niš, Serbia
{milena.frtunic.gligorijevic,darko.puflovic,
leonid.stoimenov}@elfak.ni.ac.rs
[2] Sorsix, Macedonia Office, Skopje, Republic of Macedonia
evgenija.stevanoska@sorsix.com
[3] Faculty of Medicine, University of Niš, Niš, Serbia
tjevtovic@yahoo.com
[4] Faculty of Computer Science and Engineering,
University Ss. Cyril and Methodius, Skopje, Republic of Macedonia
goran.velinov@finki.ukim.mk

Abstract. Data in the healthcare industry is overwhelming, not only because of its volume but also because of its variety. In order to use such data, it needs to be pre-processed and integrated first. An additional problem is the visualization of such big data and making it valuable, readable and easier to come to the conclusions. This paper presents a system that uses interactive maps for presenting data and services for integrating healthcare data and combining it with other external sources. The purpose of this system is to show a presence of some disease in the country, how many patients with that diagnosis had to travel to some other location in order to get the medical examination and how far they had to go. Such information can be valuable in process of organizing and optimizing healthcare resources and creating models for cheaper and more optimal healthcare both from system's and patient's perspective.

Keywords: Healthcare · Data visualization · Big data · Data integration · eHealth

1 Introduction

The adoption and use of health information technology is increasing dramatically around the world. The usage of electronic health record (EHR) systems enabled collection of a large amount of detailed medical data about the variety of patients. For that reason, there are different ways how this information can be used. For example, Accenture's Healthcare Technology Vision 2015 published a survey describing how eHealth can lead to more personalized, smarter and better health services for everyone [1]. Data generated in healthcare can be used for improving its quality, reducing costs,

© Springer International Publishing AG 2017
M. Da Silveira et al. (Eds.): DILS 2017, LNBI 10649, pp. 94–108, 2017.
https://doi.org/10.1007/978-3-319-69751-2_10

improving medical functionalities like disease surveillance and population health management [2]. Today, a majority of research is focusing on utilizing this data in a way that will lead to creating personalized healthcare systems, mechanisms for generation of new links between diseases, between symptoms and diseases, and finding ways to help doctors set up diagnosis and offer the best course of treatment.

However, healthcare data can be used not only for helping doctors and other medical personnel but for generating information that will have a direct impact on patients and help them in some way.

One of the problems in every healthcare system is making it accessible to as many people as possible. This problem can be observed not only from the financial aspect of medical services but also in terms of reducing necessary patients' commute. Geographical accessibility presents an important barrier to accessing health services. Distance and time are both important factors of accessibility [3]. If patients had to travel less in order to receive medical treatment, the overall costs would be reduced. Therefore, the healthcare would be more accessible and the system more efficient. Tackling this problem requires a thorough analysis of the system, patients and their migrations within the system.

Realization of the above analysis and processes requires data from various information systems and data sources. Such data sources contain a variety of structured, semi-structured and unstructured data than can be analyzed so that new knowledge can be discovered and healthcare system can become better and improved. Due to the data structure, volume and variety, analysis of healthcare data is very demanding and requires data pre-processing.

Data visualization has become a powerful tool in analyzing such data [4]. Conventional tools (such as tables) lack functionality and usability because of the quantity of the information that needs to be presented and analyzed. For that reason, even some well-known solutions for data visualization are not giving enough functionality for analyzing data from all domains. Some data analysis requires custom tools for specific problems and healthcare datasets are one of them.

Because of that, this paper proposes an interactive map visualization system that integrates semi-structured and structured healthcare data from different locations combines them with external sources and visualizes them on the map. The purpose of this solution is to give a readable preview on the presence of different diseases in the country and all patients' migrations in order to facilitate deducting conclusions about optimal usage of the healthcare system. Moreover, it can help in concluding if there are possibilities to make the health services more efficient, more accessible and less expensive for both patients and healthcare industry.

2 Healthcare Big Data Analysis and Visualization

Healthcare systems contain many branches where each of them has its own specifics and different type of data that needs to be stored. Information from these systems can be kept in different forms and volume, usually semi-structured and incomplete. Because of that, the creation of systems that use this data for analyses has many problems. Two main problems that were addressed in this paper in process of designing this prototype were: a problem of gathering and pre-processing data and problem of choosing the best way to visualize results of analyses.

2.1 Data Pre-processing

Data collected in hospitals is stored in databases that mostly can't be used for analysis and research purposes. These databases are used for storing data that is necessary for normal functioning of hospitals and they contain large quantities of sensitive information. Accessing this information have to be authorized and should not produce unnecessary delay to the entire system. The emphasis is on data protection and unobstructed system functioning, so information needed for research from those databases can be distributed to researchers in some of the formats used to store raw data, like CSV, TSV, JSON, XML and many others. Even more useful knowledge can be gathered from other sources, like web pages or other text documents that are semi-structured [5]. Patient data is not of much use unless it is combined with other sources. Unlike mentioned files, that have structure, data that can be obtained from web pages is in most cases in semi-structured format. Some examples of such data are information about population, divided by gender or combined, distances between cities or travel times. Also, some of these data may also be in unstructured format, like missing information about clinics and pharmacies. Updating information about business hours can be easy using information from their website. It is not an easy task to access information stored in these formats so it is necessary to prepare that data for further use first.

Data preparation consists of several steps [6, 7]. Raw data usually contain incorrect values and duplicates because data entry in hospitals can suffer from human errors or technical issues so it is essential to remove them as well as to fill in the missing information if it is possible to infer their real value. The processing of healthcare information involves the use of different sources that usually contain a lot of redundant data so integration step has to address these issues and produce datasets that contain only the data needed for analysis. Except for file types that can be used as input, formats used to store data itself can be different and before its proper use, it is necessary to provide storage in the same format throughout entire dataset. After those steps, data is almost ready for analysis, but still, consist of values that are not needed for analysis, so it is important to remove unnecessary data, which is crucial for faster and easier analysis, but also of great importance for data security.

Even after removal of all the unnecessary data, the quantity of information is overwhelming and there is a need to use data storage system. Column based data store is increasingly popular in situations where priority is to store data efficiently and to allow fast search using only small number of columns from the entire dataset [8]. Information stored in this way does not keep duplicate values, but rather combines identical values with the list of all row identifiers which contain that value. In the case of medical records, where a lot of column values contain identical information this approach can save a lot of space, but also allow much faster query times. Using entire rows from the database is rarely needed, especially during the lookups so column based approach can save a lot of time.

Data storage format that column-based databases use enables usage of SIMD instructions [9]. Queries over healthcare data mostly use simple operations on a large number of values stored in few columns. Entire columns can be stored in memory without the need to access other ones. After data is in memory, it is easy to execute simple operations over large datasets at once and to enable parallelization, because reading of the necessary data needed for analysis is now based on sample sequential scans.

Column-oriented databases allow different compression methods to be used depending on the structure of columns and database itself. This way, it is possible to use compression methods that can't be used in traditional databases, because every column can use a different technique, which enables the use of approaches based on data type, whether it is sorted beforehand or based on the similarity found in the column [10]. On the other hand, decompression of columns used in queries is not needed until values from them have to be returned for presentation. Only values from columns that are needed have to be decompressed, that saves CPU time.

2.2 Healthcare Data Visualization

Big data is high volume, high velocity, and high variety datasets whose value lies in understanding the data and generating new knowledge. Data visualization has become an important component of big data analytics since it allows users to see more infor-mation at the same time. Graph, diagram or chart visualization has proven to be more efficient than analysis of long spreadsheets of reports. Moreover, the volume of Big Data is making conventional analyzing tools nonfunctional since it is very hard to read such huge amount of data and the overload of the information may lead to overlooking and misinterpreting crucial information. For that reason, many traditional business intelligence and analytics vendors and some new market entrants are offering new data visualization technologies and platforms. There are few commercial solutions on the market, like Tableau[1], Qlik[2] and Silk[3] that offer different possibilities for Big Data visualization by using a variety of diagrams, images, charts and many other interactive methods.

However, when visualizing Big Data it is very important to choose proper data representation, since not all visualization techniques are appropriate for all purposes [11]. Some techniques give better results for some problems and there are some fields where general solutions are simply not good enough.

Main research tasks for this paper were choosing the best way for presenting migrations that exist in the system, choosing how the grouping should be done and how data should be classified while maintaining results readable and clear.

Healthcare information systems have data-related problems similar to those in other domains. However, this discipline has a number of domain-specific challenges, from a large number of patients, large numbers of heterogeneous variables, data linking across

---

[1] Tableau - https://www.tableau.com/.

[2] Qlik - http://www.qlik.com/us/.

[3] Silk - https://www.silk.co/.

multiple sources and missing or incomplete data, to a great number of domains where visualization focus can be put [12]. West et al. gave a review of different approaches in visualizing data and the current state of the art visualization techniques that have been used with EHR data [13]. In the recent years, many papers have discussed problems in healthcare visualization and most of them have done a research targeting specific healthcare-related research problems [14, 15].

The majority of papers have focused on using information visualization and visual analytics for improving patient treatment by creating personalized healthcare for every patient and a better preview of patient's electronic health record. Moreover, they have focused on finding new patterns and links between diseases and symptoms in order to improve healthcare overall. For this purpose, visualization is usually supported by zoom, filter and overview options as key components of interactive data visualization which is found to be the most suitable visualization technique.

Interactive data visualization technique translates data from its original format to graphic presentation dynamically. The main advantages of this approach are [11]:

- Possibility for users to switch between multiple data sources.
- Interactive data visualization can present both detailed macro information and aggregated information within a single preview. Users can see the overall picture and details for every record with its links.
- These techniques are effective for describing multiple states and how they transit from one to another in a complex system.
- Easy to understand and has visual impact. Hotspots are transparent.

Geographic Information Systems (GIS) are powerful tools for analyzing and displaying any geospatial data and revealing and examining geographic relations between data in a certain domain. GIS has been used to assess health care needs, analyze access to health services and understand disparities in access among different groups, evaluate health care utilization and its geographical variations and plan and evaluate health services [16]. Today, there are many frameworks, mapping tools and libraries that offer different possibilities for presenting data on the map, starting with Google API[4], Leaflet[5], D3.js[6], OpenLayers[7] and many others.

Because of the above-stated benefits, it was decided to go forewarned with maps in combination with interactive visualization for showing migrations and other information.

3 Interactive Map Visualization System

This paper proposes a specialized system for gathering, pre-processing, storing, analyzing and visualizing healthcare data on interactive map. The system integrates healthcare data from different sources and combines them with external resources in

---

[4] Google Maps API - https://developers.google.com/maps/.

[5] Leaflet - http://leafletjs.com/.

[6] D3.js - https://d3js.org/.

[7] OpenLayers - https://openlayers.org/.

order to generate better data overview and new knowledge. The purpose of this solution is to show the presence of some disease in different locations as well as patient's migrations and statistical information. The overall architecture of the system is presented in Fig. 1. As it can be seen, the system consists of two independent units:

- Data pre-processing system – system for healthcare data integration from different sources, preparation and importation into database represented using DB component in the system's architecture.
- Data visualization system – system that integrates healthcare data with external sources and visualizes them on an interactive map.

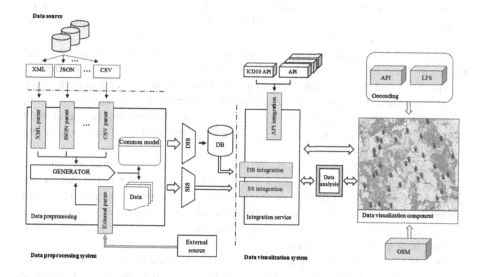

Fig. 1. System's architecture

3.1 Data Pre-processing System Component

Data pre-processing system gathers data from healthcare institutions and other external sources like HTML pages that may contain valuable information for further steps of analysis. Data generated in the data pre-processing system is later used by data visualization system for analysis and visualization on the map. The communication between the systems is done through database that is in the middle of the system.

One way to ensure patient anonymity is to replace real values with special numeric values that point to them. Medical data usually contain a lot of those values stored along with real information and mappings between them. This makes data more secure and saves a lot of space, but dumps that contain those numeric values are not suitable for further analysis until they are replaced with subset of original information. Original information is often stored in dictionaries, but it can be in variety of formats as well. Database systems usually do not support most of them, and transformation into format that is interpretable by the system can take a lot of time.

However, any of those formats contain column descriptions and names alongside real values that can be used to transform them into common model. The Common model is created using .NET Compiler Platform[8], open source compiler for C# and Visual Basic .NET programming languages. Scripting capabilities of .NET compiler platform can transform common model and raw data into objects in memory on runtime and use them later directly from service or store to the database. Using the appropriate parser, it is possible not only to gather data from the files but also use this data to collect important information about them, which later can be used to create a more accurate model. This way, it is possible not only to replace all the numeric values with their real counterparts, but also to check for unreliable, incorrect or missing records. Another advantage of this approach is the possibility of expanding to other data types. Parts of the system that are responsible for fetching data are organized as extensions. New extensions that can read other data formats can be written easily and added to the system.

Common model names and types are in most cases inferred from the file structure inside raw data. In situations where this is not possible, generator can recommend generic names and types capable of storing all the data and user is able to change any part of the schema. Even in cases when there is no information about names and types, generator provides useful information about structure of the data that can be of great help, especially when dealing with large files and a large amount of information that contains incorrect values.

Not all information is important for analysis, especially after replacing numeric with real values. Using common model it is easy to filter out all the values that are not needed for further analysis or even perform simple transformations on them which will convert them into more suitable forms. This reduction step is important to enable faster analysis, reduce the amount of space required for storage, but also for security reasons, knowing how sensitive this information is.

Once the common model layout is inferred, it can be used to help in the process of creating the database scheme and transferring data to the database through database importation system (DIS) or it can be used directly, combined with data, through service importation system (SIS). Large raw files can't be transferred at once, but have to be divided into smaller chunks and this can easily be achieved using the common model by converting parts of text from the files to objects which can be stored or consumed directly.

Advantages that column based database provide compared to other systems which are listed in chap. 2.1, are of great importance for this solution and narrowed the list of the potential data storage systems to Hypertable[9]. Ignoring cloud-based systems due to the nature of the data we are dealing with, there were other solutions that could be applied. Analysis that need to be performed over data consist of a series of reduce operations over all data stored mostly in one or two columns. Due to this, the processing speed is much higher using column based rather than the graph databases. Usage of the graph databases remain one of the possible improvements in the future, if it becomes necessary to pay more attention to the arrangement of the connections

---

[8] .NET Compiler Platform - https://github.com/dotnet/roslyn.

[9] Hypertable - http://www.hypertable.org/.

between patients and their movement. However, because of the way Hypertable stores and sorts the data is offering fast access that is very important for analytical tasks, this system was chosen for data storage. In case of tracking patient's movement, sorted patient identifiers, that represent row keys according to which the data is sorted [17], can be used to allow almost instant data access and usage of much simpler queries. Performance is at the appropriate level for this task and data visualization does not suffer because of the data access speed. Although the system does not offer security measures at the level of other systems, Hypertable is open source solution and it is possible to install it on a local computer that will allow access to the database through the security layer provided by a service which enables the use of more sophisticated methods of protection.

A very important feature of Hypertable, unlike Apache Cassandra for example, is the absence of data types, but also the presence of the quantifier field that accepts any type of information and enables its use in queries. In this way, it is possible to enter any information and store it as a value, but also enter information about data type of that value if necessary and store it as a quantifier. The values are stored as a sequence of bytes, so it is possible to convert any type of data into its binary representation and store that value into the database, but also to convert it back to its original value during reading from the database, thanks to information about type stored in the quantifier field. Reading data row by row from the raw data does not allow knowing data type of the column in advance because parts of the file can contain information that uses different ones, but in this case that is not a problem, because one column can accommodate many different types, and then the application can determine what procedure is going to be used in case of invalid data. This is often the case with identifiers, which are mostly numbers, but it is impossible to know in advance whether it is enough to store them as 32-bit or 64-bit numbers. Even more difficult is to predict all the possible types of invalid entries hidden in the raw file, such as "NA", "NaN" and many others. In this way, it is also possible to save space needed for data storage because most types don't need to be stored as a UTF-8 string, which can lead to serious savings in disk space that is required.

This system also offers excellent support for data input via file, which is extremely important when dealing with large raw files. The common model can be used to translate the raw file into TSV format that Hypertable accepts as input, which contains information about the column names, quantifiers and values themselves, so that most information that model contained is not lost, but transformed into a format suitable for the system. Translation into TSV files is simple and mostly similar to the process of translating to the common model itself. This approach is much faster than the sequential entry of individual information.

Another positive thing about Hypertable is the ability to use a variety of programming languages and the most common operating systems. API is easy to use, provides quick access and loading data from the database that is one more thing that positively influences the response and performance of the whole system.

3.2   Data Visualization Component

Data visualization component is part of the proposed system that is in charge of integrating healthcare datasets with other sources and visualizing results on the map. This component consists of two parts: one is service for data integration and preparation and other is data visualization.

The part that is in charge of data integration (Integration service) presents a WCF service that gathers and combines data from other external sources and healthcare data that is stored in this system's database. It enables access to all information that is important for visualization. The service is built to communicate with different sources and can be easily expanded in order to support more resources. This component is completely independent of any other part of the system and gives support to the visualization component. It has interfaces for communication with visualization component, system's database and external resources. It uses DB integration component to communicate with the database and read healthcare data and API component to include external services that could be valuable for analyses.

At this point, free ICD10 codes API[10] is integrated as external source resource in the system. ICD-10 is the 10th revision of the International Statistical Classification of Diseases and Related Health Problems which contains all codes for all diseases hierarchic organized into groups of similar diseases. Healthcare datasets do not have relationships between ICD 10 codes, every entry contains internal code which consists information for ICD10 code. For that reason, information that is gathered through this API is used as source information for classifying diseases appearing in the system into groups of related diseases and generating hierarchical information for all of them. This is done by taking part or complete ICD 10 code from healthcare data and searching it in the ICD10 codes database. Also, the system uses this information in order to offer its users possibility to choose the disease or group of diseases they want to analyze.

Integration service is easily expandable and has a possibility to include more external sources and combine its data with existing information in order to offer better analysis and more options for visualization to the users. Within this service, SS integration (Service System Integration) is designed to read any external sources by using communication with SIS (Service Importation System) from data importation component. In combination with service for automatic information parsing, this service can gather resources from almost any source with no difference if data is structured or semi-structured. Parsing component can transform this data into a common model which, after that, can be paired with the data obtained from the database or already existing services in order to offer better service.

Between integration service and data visualization component, there is Data analyses block that is in charge of running statistical analysis and machine learning algorithms on the integrating data and sending results to the visualization component to be presented to the users. At this point, it is limited to statistical analysis only, with tendency be expanded with machine learning algorithms. Both, information from

---

[10] IDC10 code API - https://www.hipaaspace.com/.

integration service and data analysis block are sent to the visualization component to be presented to the user.

3.3   Implementation of Data Visualization Component

Data visualization component is a Web application that communicates only with integration service in order to obtain information. This component is an Ajax-based application that uses OpenStreetMap[11] (OSM in the architecture) as the source for maps, Leaflet framework for manipulation with geospatial data, D3.js and Chart.js libraries for generating and presenting diagrams and charts.

Since data in the healthcare systems is not geo-referenced, in order to present the result on the map, this component uses Geocoding for generating geo-information for the results. Geocoding module in the architecture uses MapQuest Geocoding API[12] in combination with local resources (LFS in the architecture). The local resource is building over time and presents the first resource for finding geo-information for the location. If the resource does not contain the match, the MapQuest API is called. In order to make this process as optimal as possible, each time when a new call to the MapQuest Geocoding API is made, a copy of the result is saved in the LFS. This is done in order to avoid multiple API calls for the same location and save time that is needed for data preparation in the visualization process.

Data visualization component offers users possibility to analyze healthcare data gathered from EHR system by communicating with Data integration component. It gives users opportunity to search and filter data based on ICD10 codes and to choose one or more diseases they want to analyze. Filtration starts from the most general ICD 10 codes groups. One can choose one or more groups. After that, the user can filter his choice more specifically by selecting subcategories of the chosen ICD 10 group. If he wants, he can go one level further and filter the next level of subcategories for all of his choices in order to get more specific results. At any filter level, the user can stop filtration and analyze group results for all selected categories and diseases within them.

Visualization map maps all places where patients that correspond to the filtered setup live along with statistics that correspond to the filter. The statistics contain information about the total number of patients, number of patients that had to migrate to receive health service, number of migration, number of clinics that were visited, average distance that patients had to cover. Further, statistics shows information about both number of patients and migrations that traveled to another municipality and number of patients and migrations that traveled to another region. An example of such preview is shown in Fig. 2. In order to get better performance and to solve a problem of huge amount of data, every selection loads new data only when it is needed to be presented on the map. The user can see summary information and then navigate to the more specific results. For every location, one can see the total number of patients, how many had to travel in order to be treated and where did they have to go. This information is shown both graphically on charts and on the map by drawing migration

---

[11] OpenStreetMap - https://www.openstreetmap.org/.

[12] MapQuest Geocoding API - https://developer.mapquest.com/documentation/geocoding-api/.

routes between places. For every migration, the user can see how many patients traveled to each place in order to get treated. In order to get a more informative overview, the system uses interactive map visualization which is reflected in interactive changes of layers displayed on the map.

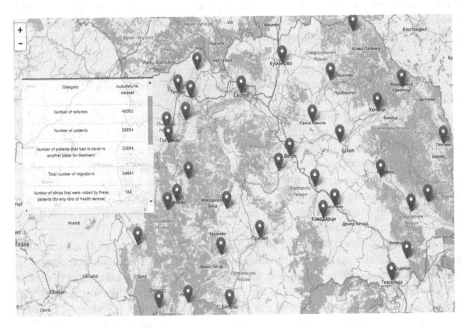

Fig. 2. Example of all places where patients with the same disease live

Once the user chooses a specific place that he wants to analyze, summary information layer gets removed from the preview and only individual information is shown. An example of all migrations from one place is shown in Fig. 3. As it can be seen, once the user selects a place for analysis all migrations from chosen place are shown followed by the corresponding chart with overall information and statistical data. Summary information presents all places and numbers of patients per place. The red dot on the map present chosen place and blue markers present all locations where patients with selected diseases traveled to. The user has the possibility to select any marker and see the information for that specific place, name, percentage and number of patients that came there from the selected location and how far it is from the patients' hometown.

Such visualization gives a clear preview of the overall situation in the healthcare system and can be a valuable asset in the analysis of the presence of some diseases and weather there are a lot of migrations for them in some areas. It can even be used to determine how far patients had to travel and if those distances could be shorter.

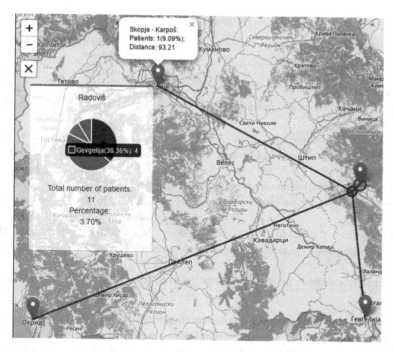

Fig. 3. Example of summary information for patients for one place and their migrations

4   Conclusion

The presented system was tested with data from Macedonian healthcare system which contains 2741 clinics, 7666 doctors and serves ∼95% of citizens that are insured by the fund and have access to the public healthcare sector [18]. Data used for testing the proposed solution was imported from EHR System MojTermin (MyAppointment) [18]. For testing all functionalities the system used sample of 2204673 prescriptions and 454521 referrals for April, 2016. This dataset was used only to determine if all functionalities work correctly. Additionally, system was tested with larger datasets (that gives more realistic load) for cancer and autoimmune diseases for 3 year period (2014–2016). The following Table 1 gives a summary of used datasets and statistical information calculated by the proposed system.

This data used for testing is another indicator that reduces patients' commute could have a big impact (having for example 66% of autoimmune patients had to travel on average 107 km for their medical services). Visualization of these migrations could help in determining how they look like and if they can be optimized.

The presented system is a prototype that can be used for planning the optimization and improvement of the whole healthcare system. It gives a clear preview of points where some optimization may be needed. Such improvement can be extremely valu-

Table 1. Testing dataset characteristics

Category	Autoimmune dataset	Cancer dataset
Number of referrals	48063	620466
Number of patients	29854	124032
Number of patients that had to travel to another place for treatment	20854	96347
Total number of migrations	34641	474552
Number of clinics that were visited by these patients (for any kind of health service)	184	260
Number of patients that had to travel to other municipalities	18900	90963
Number of migrations for patients that had to travel to other municipalities	32077	447383
Number of patients that had to travel to other regions	6903	40035
Number of migrations for patients that had to travel to other regions	12629	204764
Average traveling distance for all patients that had to travel	107 km	97 km

able for patients since it can make migrations shorter which will lead to saving patient's time. Also, with adequate systems' optimization, waiting time can be reduced and overall cost of the treatments may become more economical. This way, the healthcare system will be more affordable to many people.

At this point, the system integrates data only from one external source – ICD10 codes hierarchy; it shows the presence of diseases in the area; and all patients' migrations. However, since it is built to be easily expandable and all modules are independent and have expandable interfaces for communication with other components in the system, the plan is to combine existing data with other external sources in order to offer more possibilities for analysis.

The first version of this system is relying on data imported from other systems. If some data is missing, like information about the location, that record will be discarded and won't be processed. This is an issue that should be further explored and requires implementation of an algorithm that will fulfill missing location data so that all data is processed. This problem will be addressed in the next faze of development together with improving visualization component by adding new features like different line thicknesses that will indicate travel frequencies.

The plan is to include support for more data sources that can be used and for more types of healthcare data that can be imported into the system in order to provide more reliable results. Since the expectations are the volume of data in the system is going to grow rapidly, the plan is also to transform data storage into the cluster structure. This change is going to allow more data to be stored without compromising system's performance. Further, data analysis component in the visualization system will be expanded with predictive algorithms, machine learning algorithms and movement models in order to provide more informative and useful system for analysis.

References

1. Safavi, K., Ratli, R.: Top 5 eHealth Trends. Healthcare IT Vision. Accenture (2015)
2. Feldman, B., Martin, E., Skotnes, T.: Big Data in Healthcare Hype and Hope. Dr. Bonnie 360° (2012)
3. Munoz, U.H., Källestål, C.: Geographical accessibility and spatial coverage modeling of the primary health care network in the Western Province of Rwanda. Int. J. Health Geographics **11**(1), 40 (2012). BioMed Central Ltd.
4. Keim, D.A.: Information visualization and visual data mining. IEEE Trans. Vis. Comput. Graph. **8**(1), 1–8 (2002). IEEE
5. Lai, Y., Salgueiro, F., Stone, D.: Integrating Non-clinical Data with EHRs. In: Secondary Analysis of Electronic Health Records, pp. 51–60. Springer, Cham (2016). doi:10.1007/978-3-319-43742-2_6
6. Danziger, J., Zimolzak, A.J.: Residual confounding lurking in big data: a source of error. In: Secondary Analysis of Electronic Health Records, pp. 71–78. Springer, Cham (2016). doi:10.1007/978-3-319-43742-2_8
7. Pyle, D.: Data Preparation for Data Mining. Morgan Kaufmann Publishers Inc., San Francisco (1999)
8. Begoli, E., Dunning, T., Frasure, C.: Real-time discovery services over large, heterogeneous and complex healthcare datasets using schema-less, column-oriented methods. In: IEEE Second International Conference on Big Data Computing Service and Applications (BigDataService), pp. 257–264. IEEE, Oxford (2016)
9. Abadi, D., Boncz, P., Harizopoulos, S., Idreos, S., Madden, S.: The design and implementation of modern column-oriented database systems. Found. Trends Databases **5**(3), 197–280 (2013). Now Publishers Inc., Breda
10. Abadi, D., Madden, S., Ferreira, M.: Integrating compression and execution in column-oriented database systems. In: Yu, C., Scheuermann, P., Chaudhuri, S. (eds.) Proceedings of the 2006 ACM SIGMOD International Conference on Management of Data, 27–29 June, Chicago, IL, USA (2006)
11. Wang, L., Wang, G., Alexander, C.: Big data and visualization: methods, challenges and technology progress. Digit. Technol. **1**(1), 33–38 (2015). Science and Education Publishing, Newark, US
12. Gotz, D., Borland, D.: Data-Driven healthcare: challenges and opportunities for interactive visualization. IEEE Comput. Graph. Appl. **3**(1) (2017). IEEE Computer Society, Washington, US
13. West, V., Borland, D., Hammond, E.: Innovative information visualization of electronic health record data: a systematic review. J. Am. Med. Inform. Assoc. **22**(2), 330–339 (2015). Oxford University Press, Oxford
14. Shneiderman, B., Plaisant, C., Hesse, B.: Improving healthcare with interactive visualization. Computer **46**(5), 58–66 (2013). IEEE, Washington
15. Caban, J., Gotz, D.: Visual analytics in healthcare: opportunities and research challenges. J. Am. Medical Informatics Assoc. **22**, 260–262 (2015). Oxford University Press, Oxford, UK
16. McLafferty, S.L.: GIS and health care. Ann. Rev. Public Health **24**, 25–42 (2003). Annual Reviews

17. Shen, Y., Li, Y., Wu, L., Liu, S., Wen, Q.: Big Data techniques, tools, and applications. In: Enabling the New Era of Cloud Computing: Data Security, Transfer, and Management, pp. 185–212. IGI Global, Hershey (2013)
18. Velinov, G., Jakimovski, B., Lesovski, D., Ivanova Panova, D., Frtunik, D., Kon-Popovska, M.: EHR System MojTermin: Implementation and Initial Data Analysis, Studies in health technology and informatics, vol. 210, pp. 872–876. IOS Press (2015)

Author Index

Printed in the United States
By Bookmasters